Discount Travel Wisdom

Discount Travel Wisdom

Your Travel Planning and Discount Guide

Elaine Ktistes, CTC

K Travel Press
Long Island City, NY

This publication is designed as a source of authoritative information about travel planning. Every effort has been made to offer you the most accurate and current information possible. At no time shall the author or publisher be responsible or liable for misinterpretation, inaccuracy, or changes in the travel industry. Because of the instability in the travel industry, changes may occur at any time and affect information presented. It is in your best interest to seek the advice of a travel professional.

Published by K Travel Press
Long Island City, NY 11104

Publisher's Cataloging-in-Publication Data
Ktistes, Elaine.
Discount travel wisdom : your travel planning and discount guide
Elaine Ktistes. — Long Island City, NY : K Travel Press, 2003.

p. ; cm.
ISBN 0-9725333-0-3

1. Travel—Planning—Handbooks, manuals, etc. I. Title

G153.4 K85	2003	2002114274
910.2	—dc21	0103

Cover design by Kelli Leader
Cover concept by Elaine Ktistes
Interior design by Debbie Sidman/Paw Print Media
Interior artwork/cartoons courtesy of *www.arttoday.com*
Edited by Stella Ramsay

Project Coordination by Jenkins Group, Inc. www.bookpublishing.com

Printed in the United States of America

07 06 05 04 03 • 5 4 3 2 1

For the latest information about travel websites
send an e-mail to
tips@discounttravelwisdom.com

Contents

Acknowledgments xv
Introduction xvii

Part One: Preplanning 1

Overview 2

CHAPTER 1 Preplanning Step 1: The Travelers 3
Traveling With Several People 4
Types of Documentation 5
Types of Government Documentation 5
U.S. Government-Issued Identification 6
Figure 1.1 STEP 1: The Travelers 9

CHAPTER 2 Preplanning Step 2: The Importance of Timing 11
When Do You Want to Go? 12
How Long Will You Be Away? 12
Timing Affects Where You Can Go 13
When Should You Make Your Reservations? 14
Figure 2.1 STEP 2: When Do You Want to Go? 16

CHAPTER 3 Preplanning Step 3: What Do You Want to Do on Vacation? 17

Need vs. Desires 18

Figure 3.1 *STEP 3: What Do You Want to Do There?* 20

CHAPTER 4 Preplanning Step 4: Where Do You Want to Go? 23

What Affects Where You Can Go: 23

Tips to Help You Decide Where to Go: 24

Tips on Selecting a Destination 25

Step 4: How to Determine Where to Go 26

Figure 4.1 *STEP 4: How to Determine Where to Go* 27

CHAPTER 5 Preplanning Step 5: Budget and Payments 29

Tips to Keep Your Costs Under Control 29

How Will You Pay for Your Trip? 30

A Word about Credit Cards 31

Those Hidden Charges 32

Tips to Save Money 35

Figure 5.1 *STEP 5: How Will You Pay for Your Trip?* 36

Figure 5.2 *Trip Estimates* 37

CHAPTER 6 Preplanning Step 6: How to Get There 41

Summary Part One: Preplanning 42

Figure 6.1 *Preplanning Summary Sheet* 43

Figure 6.2 *Group Summary Sheet* 44

Part Two: Gathering Information 47

CHAPTER 7 Research You Must Do 49

Review Your Guidelines 49

How to Do Research 49

Research: How to Get There 54

Part Three: All About Airlines 57

CHAPTER 8 Understanding the Airline Industry 59
The Airline Route System 59
"No Frills" or Discount Airlines 61
"No Frills" General Information 63
International "No Frills" Airlines 66

CHAPTER 8.1 Airline Hub and Spoke System 69
What Is a Hub City? 69
Tips for Cheaper Airfares 70
Benefits and Disadvantages of a Hub and Spoke System 70
List of Hub Cities 71
If Airlines Sold Paint *72*

CHAPTER 8.2 Anatomy of an Airfare 74
Travel Agent's GDS Computer Screen 75
What Is a Nonrefundable Airfare? 76
General Rules of Nonrefundable Airfares 77
Summary of Nonrefundable Rules 81
Understanding the Electronic Ticket Process 81
Benefits of an Electronic Ticket 82
Disadvantages of Electronic Tickets 83

CHAPTER 8.3 Surf the Web for Airfares 84
Where Should You Begin? 85
Sidestep.com's Plug-in Browser 87
Other Travel Search Engines 89
Travel Agency Computer Systems 93
Bidding for Airline Tickets 93
Handicaps of Using the Web 94
Tips for Surfing the Web 95

CHAPTER 8.4 Sources for Airline Discounts 96

CHAPTER 8.5 How to Make an Airline Reservation 107
Review Established Guidelines 107
Research 107
Choosing a Booking Source 108
Book It 108
Write Information Down 109
Proofread Your Written Confirmation 109
Figure 8.5 Airline Reservation Sheet 110

Part Four: How To's for Hotels 111

CHAPTER 9 Overview of Hotels 113
Types of Hotels 114
Quality of Your Hotel 115
Determining the True Quality of a Hotel 116
Chain Hotels 117
Generic Hotel Rating System 117
Why Do Rates Vary? 118
Hotel and Room Features 119
Figure 9.0 Hotel Check Off List 120

CHAPTER 9.1 What Is Included in the Room Rate 123
Room Rates and Categories 123
Types of Rates 123
Per Night Rates vs. Prepaid Package Rate 124
Those Extra Charges 125
A Note about Tipping 127

CHAPTER 9.2 Determining Your Basic Hotel Needs 128
Determining Your Bare Bones Needs 128
How Will You Use Your Hotel Room? 128

What Will You Do on Vacation? 129
Hotel Location and Getting Around 129

CHAPTER 9.3 Hotel Research 130
How to Select a Hotel 130
Sources for Hotel Research 130
Almost Ready to Book Your Hotel 131
Ways to Book Your Hotel Room 132
Ways to Hold Your Reservation 132
Verify Cancellation Policies 133
A Note About Dates for Hotel Stays 133
Hotel Booking Check List 134
Which Booking Source Will You Use? 135
Sample Hotel Research 135
How to Find an Economical Hotel 136
***Figure 9.3** Hotel Reservation Sheet 138*

CHAPTER 9.4 Surf the Web for Hotels 140
Where to Surf First 140
Bidding for Hotel Rooms on the Web 143
How Bidding Works for Hotels 144
Last-Minute Travel 145
Handicaps of Using the Web for Hotels 145
Tips for Surfing the Web for Hotels 145

CHAPTER 9.5 Sources for Hotel Discounts 147
Hotel Reservation Savvy 147
Tips for Getting a Lower Rate 148
Type of Discounts 149
Tips for Finding Hard-to-Get Rooms 152

Part Five: Choosing Car Rentals 153

CHAPTER 10 Choosing Car Rentals 155
You Must Have a Credit Card to Rent a Car 155
How Big a Car Should You Rent? 156
Car Rental Rates 156
Those Extra Charges 157
What Is the Collision Damage Waiver? 158
Should You Buy Collision Damage Coverage? 159
How Does This Differ from Liability Insurance? 159
Should You Buy Supplemental Liability Insurance? 159
Should You Buy PAI—Personal Accident Insurance? 160
Should You Buy PEC—Personal Effects Insurance? 160
Back to that Collision Damage Waiver 160
Credit Card Coverage 160
When Is Your Credit Card Benefit Valid? 162
Be Wary of Scams 162
A Story About Gasoline 163
Money-Saving Tips 164
Trip Cancellation Insurance: Should You Buy It? 166

CHAPTER 10.1 Car Rental Discounts 166
Compare Rates Among Booking Sources 166
Tips for Surfing the Web for Cars 168
Sources for Car Discounts 168
International Car Discounts 169
Last-Minutes Specials 170

Part Six: Should You Buy a Package? 171

CHAPTER 11 Packages, Tours, and All-Inclusives 173
What Are Packages, Tours, and All-Inclusives? 174

Some Notes About Packages 174
Why Buy a Package or Tour? 175
How to Buy a Package or Tour 175
If You Decide to Buy a Package from a Travel Agent 175
Questions You Should Ask 176
Surfing the Web for Packages 177
What Is a Travel Deal? 177
Last Minute Packages and Travel Deals 178
All Inclusives: Pros and Cons 179
Insurance: Should You Buy It? 180

Part Seven: Exploring Your Booking Options 181

CHAPTER 12 Exploring Your Booking Options 183
Consumer Booking Patterns 183
Should You Do It Yourself? 184
Know When You Are Over Your Head and Turn to a Travel Agent 185
What a Travel Agent Can Do for You 185
General Services Provided 186

CHAPTER 12.1 About Travel Agents 188
Types of Travel Agencies 188
Types of Travel Agents 191
What Kind of Travel Agent Do You Need? 192
How to Find a Reliable Travel Agent 193
Getting a Good Deal 195
Service Fees 195s

CHAPTER 12.2 Doing It Yourself 198
Steps For Doing It Yourself 198

Part Eight: What to Do After You Buy Your Ticket 201

CHAPTER 13 Travel Documents 203
Document Check List 203
Other Stuff Check List 204

CHAPTER 13.1 Airport Check-In Procedures 205
Running the Check-In Gauntlet 205
Airline Ticket Counter Check In 205
Airport Security Tips 207
Gate Check In 208
Car Rental Check In 209

Part Nine: Rules, Changes, and Refunds 211

CHAPTER 14 What to Do If You Can't Go 213
Basic Rules for Nonrefundable Tickets 213
Making Changes to Nonrefundable Tickets 214
Changing the Return Flight of a Nonrefundable Ticket 216
If the Flight You Want Is Sold Out, What Do You Do? 217
Changes for Other Than Nonrefundable Tickets 218
Refunding Full-Fare Tickets 219

Part Ten: How To's for Frequent Flyers 221

CHAPTER 15 Frequent Flyer Miles 223
What Are Frequent Flyer Miles? 223
How to Accrue/Collect Miles 223
Other Ways to Accrue Frequent Flyer Miles 225
Benefits of Frequent Flyer Miles 226
Best Use of Your Frequent Flyer Miles 227
How to Redeem Your Miles 228

Step One: Do You Have Enough Miles? 228
Step Two: Check Seat Availability 230
Step Three: Make Your Reservation 231
Step Four: Order Your Award Coupon 232
If You Need to Order Your Frequent Flyer Award 232
Step Five: Redeem Award Certificate and Issue Airline Ticket 233
Step Six: Written Confirmation of Itinerary 233
Step Seven: Look Over the Itinerary Immediately 234
Changing Dates and Cities After the Certificate Is Redeemed 234
Noteworthy Tips 235
Figure 15.1 *Frequent Flyer Steps* *236*

Appendix **237**

GLOSSARY Industry Lingo **239**
Hotel Phone Numbers and Websites *245*
Car Rental Phone Numbers and Websites *247*
Ordering Information *248*
Vacation Request Form *249*

About the Author 250

Acknowledgments

Many people have been supportive and helpful during the writing of *Discount Travel Wisdom*. Those I mention here have made a difference in its outcome.

Leah Nicholson, production coordinator from Bookpublishing.com has been my guide and anchor through the publishing process. **Debbie Sidman**, interior designer, lightened the tone of the book from technical to less serious/whimsy with the use of cartoons. Also a double thanks to Debbie for rescuing the book cover by finding a cover image that works. **Bonnie Kogos**, friend, author, and fellow travel agent, has held me together when I was ready to quit by telling me I'm great and have information the public needs. And, to **Stella Ramsay**, my wonderfully talented editor, who made the technical writing easier to read.

My most important and supportive being, **Alley**, the cat with more sense than her owner. My furry alarm clock would religiously remind me to take a break by sleeping atop my research papers and laying her head on my laptop's enter key.

Acknowledgments

Introduction

When I started in the travel business in 1973, there were 3 airfares: first class, regular coach, and a discounted/excursion (DA30) fare whose only rule was that you could stay up to a maximum of 30 days. We got all of our information out of a book, the OAG, Official Airline Guide. The domestic version contained the flight schedules of all airlines flying in/out of a domestic U.S. or Canadian airport AND all the airfares of each routing. When there were 3 airfares, this could be done. There was also a table for the breakdown of the airfare by base fare and tax. This table was 2 pages and gave amounts up to $450. There was no need for higher amounts because there was no one-way fare that exceeded $450, including first class New York City to Los Angeles. Now that one-way fare is $2103.50 and includes $155 of taxes and surcharges.

Then came computer reservation systems (CRS) and the Deregulation Act of 1983.

The airline industry changed.

And continues to change on a second-by-second basis.

In 1973, few people besides business travelers and the wealthy traveled very much. If they did, they wouldn't consider making travel arrangements without using a travel agent. Today with the advent of the Internet, savvy and not so savvy computer users feel they can make their own travel arrangements without using a travel agent. Yes, they can make airline or hotel reservations online directly through the source. But what they may be missing are the discounts and, possibly, a better itinerary.

Few people know the cost of an airline ticket or hotel room. In the first few years of *priceline.com*'s operations, a large percentage of the "name your own price" bookings were the nonrefundable airfares you could buy through normal channels: airlines, travel agents, or online. These were NOT web-only fares or any other kind of discounted airfare. People did not know they needed to research the cost of the airfare. Nor did they know how to research—whom to call or where to look on the Internet. They may not have wanted to take the time or had the time to do so in the first place. Often, what they got from *priceline.com* for the same price, were lousy departure times and lots of inconvenience. *Priceline.com* has changed its tune and now offers a check-off section that indicates off-peak times and connection guidelines. (You could still end up with an undesirable schedule.)

Today there is an enormous challenge in finding travel discounts. There can be over 25 fares between two cities, for one airline, and 22 of those fares could be for the same economy seat! Someone not using a travel agent is working blind, a kind of "hit or miss" making travel arrangements.

That is, until this book came along.

This is a book for anyone planning a trip, a guidebook both for the computer savvy Internet surfer and for someone making reservations by phone. It is especially useful for the first-time traveler. And, if you decide to work with a travel agent, you will now know what information to gather before calling them. The seasoned Internet surfer and frequent traveler can compare notes and probably find tricks, tips and discounts.

What was a simple process in 1973—look up the schedule and fare in the OAG, call the airline to book the flights and then handwrite the ticket—has now turned into an involved process even for seasoned travel agents. The variables are so numerous that even I miss a thing or two on occasion. One practically needs a law degree to decipher the airfare rules. Is the fare valid after 12 noon on Monday through 12 noon on Thursday, or only on Saturdays? But you are traveling on a Tuesday. Why is my airfare $50 more? Because that Tuesday is a holiday and is "blacked out," not offered for sale on that date. Perhaps the inventory for the cheapest fare is sold out. How do you find the lowest fare? With great difficulty and tons of research. That is the secret of this book, how to find the best fares and best schedules with the least amount of time.

Now we have the hype of "internet bargains." But how do you find them? See the tips in the chapters on surfing the web for airfares, hotels, and cars.

Not only are you wading through the quicksand of airfares, you now have to search through 20 or 30 websites, and make a million phone calls just to get some idea of pricing and availability. You are determined to spend as many hours as needed, searching the web so you can save the $50 per person fee the local travel agent is now charging to stay in business. Isn't your time worth that travel agent service fee?

If you made your reservations yourself, whom do you turn to when your plans change? No one. You have to undo all you previous work and start over, if you can. Will you remember to call all the airlines, hotels, car companies, and tour operators? How many more hours will you spend trying to undo your trip and rebook it? See the chapter on changing your trip.

In this book you will find the step-by-step process to conducting reasonable research prior to booking online or using a travel agent. These steps were developed during years of experience where I had to learn as much as possible about my client. I needed this information so I could match them with a suitable travel product. Now you have a guidebook that can help you go online and start you own travel research. Once this is done, you can enter the availability maze and attempt to book the various components of your trip—airline tickets, hotel arrangements, ground transportation, and tours. If you are overwhelmed by the choices, see the chapter on how to find a travel agent.

Elaine Ktistes, CTC
New York City

Part One: Preplanning

Chapter 1	Preplanning Step 1: The Travelers	3
Chapter 2	Preplanning Step 2: The Importance of Timing	11
Chapter 3	Preplanning Step 3: What Do You Want to Do on Vacation?	17
Chapter 4	Preplanning Step 4: Where Do You Want to Go?	23
Chapter 5	Preplanning Step 5: Budget and Payments	29
Chapter 6	Preplanning Step 6: How to Get There	41
	Summary	42

Overview

A traveler uses the travel agent for guidance and focus; otherwise, he would make his own travel arrangements. Many people have successfully made their own travel arrangements, and others don't know where to start. This book will give both the experienced traveler and the beginner the background needed to make sensible and timely decisions about discount travel.

Everyone can use some guidance when it comes to planning a vacation. A friend may have just returned from a great trip and told you all about it, showed you pictures and got you excited about going there. What you don't realize is that it was their trip with their guidelines, likes and dislikes. You need to explore your own needs and desires. Here is a way to arrange a trip that is best for you.

Preplanning is designed in 6 basic steps:

1. The travelers—who is going?
2. Timing—when are you going?
3. What activities will you do while away?
4. Where do you want to go?
5. What is your budget and how will you pay for your trip?
6. How will you get there—plane, train, ship, car, etc.?

These steps help you establish your guidelines for travel planning and choose the right options. When these 6 steps are completed, you will be focused and ready to pick up the telephone or go online. There are fill-in sheets throughout this book to help you gather your basic information and have it in one place. After you have completed the 6 steps, transfer the results to the *SUMMARY PREPLANNING SHEET*. (Located in Part One Summary section.) Then you are ready to start you research.

CHAPTER 1

Preplanning Step 1: The Travelers

You would be surprised how many people call me without considering their traveling companions. Are you traveling with your mate, children, or friends? Have you spoken to them about planning a trip? Until you have spoken to them you will not know if they want to go or if they have any requests, conflicts or objections that may affect the outcome of your travel planning.

On the fill-in sheet for STEP ONE (see Figure 1.1)

LIST THE LEGAL NAMES AND AGES OF ALL TRAVELERS, INCLUDING YOURSELF

You need to use the LEGAL names and ages. The LEGAL name is the name on the government identification you will present at check-in. See the following section, *Types of Documentation*, for specifics. The ages are a key factor when requesting discounts. Children and seniors may have special airfare discounts. Hotels may offer children sleep or eat free programs or have a children's program that might apply. Senior discounts are everywhere, especially if you are a member of AARP, the American Association of Retired Persons, (*aarp.com*). See individual chapters for airfare, hotel, or car discounts.

Also on the STEP ONE: THE TRAVELERS fill-in sheet is a list of questions that you need to consider. Check off each question when you have addressed it. The questions take into consideration several factors that could interfere with vacation planning: be sure that the dates work for everyone, including children. Consult school or work calendars, check with babysitters, caregivers, dog walkers, and anyone you would depend on while you are away. Many a trip had to be postponed because someone did not check with his or her boss for the time off. If you do this ahead of time, you can save yourself unnecessary aggravation and the added costs of rebooking fees or cancellation charges.

On the fill-in sheet, there is a section to note any frequent flyer numbers or membership associations. Note the ones you use the most. This is to give you focus later when you are choosing which airline to fly.

Traveling With Several People

If you are traveling with several people, it would be a good idea to meet several months in advance to discuss who really wants to go, how much to spend, and what activities the majority want. The dates of travel are most important. Coordinating this within a group can be tricky.

Have each family group fill out the PREPLANNING SUMMARY SHEET (located at end of PART 1) and one or two people coordinate this information onto the GROUP SUMMARY SHEET (also at the end of part one). Make several copies and give to the folks who will be doing the preliminary footwork.

- Select one or two members to do the footwork
- Report back to the group by a specific date
- Set a specific time and place for the follow-up meeting
- Go over the information gathered
- Plan about a week between meetings so you can have time to do follow-up research
- You may want to divide the footwork—one person checks out the hotels, the other the airline reservations
- Check with your travel agent or search online

Planning a vacation takes much forethought and discussion with traveling companions. Good planning makes a happy trip.

Types of Documentation

You are no doubt aware of the increased security at U.S. airports and around the world. To pass through airport security and to board your flight, the Federal Aviation Administration requires you to have valid government-issued identification card, which includes a photo of yourself. For a trip within the United States, this could be a valid state driver's license or a military I.D. See the following sections for specifics. For international trips, you will need a passport that is valid for at least 6 months. Verify if you need a visa (country authorization stamp, *not the credit card*) for your destination country.

When you are traveling, it is essential that you have all of your travel documents in an accessible place: either on your person or in your carry-on bag. Do not pack documents inside your suitcase. Often, you will be separated from your luggage. You will need your documents as you travel through various checkpoints.

Types of Government Documentation

State-Issued Driver's License: If you are traveling within the U.S., this is the identification you will need. This document:

- Must have a photograph of you on it. If your appearance has changed, i.e., you grew a beard or removed your glasses it is best to get an updated license. When you go through security at the airport, the person checking your identification must be able to match you to your picture.
- Must be in reasonable shape. If it is damaged, torn, stained, etc., your valid license might look like a forgery.

If you do not have a driver's license, proving who you are is a bit more complicated. You need a certified document along with an acceptable proof of identity with your photo on it. Company-issued picture identification or student identification can be acceptable proofs of identify. You must present a *certified birth certificate* along with either one of these.

Birth Certificates: If you do not have a driver's license, you can use an original birth certificate—one that was issued by a city agency and has the city's raised seal on it. Show this along with your picture identification: school, business, or a credit card (with picture on it).

U.S. Government-Issued Identification

U.S. Passports: If you are traveling outside of the U.S., you will need a passport and possibly a visa. U.S. passports are issued by the U.S. Department of State from the U.S. Passport Agency in the United States and overseas at a U.S. consulate. Passports are issued for 5 or 10 years, have your picture on it, and the date and place of issue, along with the very important expiration date. You can get information about passports from your local travel agency or a visa service company. Also, you can find passport information in the U.S. Government website: *http://travel.state.gov/passport_services.html.*

Tips

- The first time you apply for a passport, you will have to go in person to the passport office. You cannot send someone to do it for you. The U.S. Government requires citizens to swear allegiance. Renewal passports can be done by mail.
- Apply at least 2 months prior to traveling. In the spring, the processing time could be 4–6 weeks. If you do not have an official birth certificate (it has the raised seal on it), allow several more weeks to get that first. You need it to apply for a passport.
- Have empty pages in your passport for various country stamps and visas.
- Be current: you should have at least 6 months remaining on your passport, i.e., the expiration date is 6 months in the future. If your passport is due to expire while you are traveling, renew it prior to traveling.
- If it's a newly issued passport, sign it before you begin traveling.

- Keep it in good shape. You will not be able to travel on a passport that is damaged. If you stuck it in your back pocket and it has taken the shape of your butt, you will not be able to travel with it. You must get a new one.

Traveling to Canada: If you travel to Canada, you will require proof of citizenship to get in. It is best to bring your passport. If you don't, you will need your birth certificate and your driver's license. Otherwise, you may have a tough time getting into Canada and back into the U.S.

Traveling to Mexico: You will need your passport. If under 18 yrs old, you will need a certified letter from your parents stating whom you will travel with. Check with the Mexican consulate for details.

Visas: If you travel outside the U.S., you must check the entry requirements for the countries you plan to visit. Some countries require U.S. citizens to have a visa: a country authorization stamp, NOT the credit card. Your travel agent can easily check if a visa is needed. If you buy your airline ticket online, you may be reminded by the website that you need a visa. In any case, the responsibility of obtaining a visa is on you, not the seller of the airline ticket.

- When you check in at the airport for your INTERNATIONAL flight, the agent will then check to see if you have a valid passport and the necessary visa. If you do not have the appropriate documentation, you will not be allowed on the plane. You will not be leaving the country. You will not get your money back for your airline ticket or anything else you prepaid. You do not pass go.

- If you are connecting from another city, do not expect an airline agent there to verify your international documents. They are not required to check them. You will have your international documents checked at the airport of the departing international flight.

Some remote areas or areas under conflict may restrict travel into their country. Go to the U.S. Government's website:

http://travel.state.gov/travel_warnings.html

to see if there are any restrictions on travel, or travel warnings for the countries you want to visit. A travel agent's job is to advise you if there is a problem but may forget to check this site. Few online sites will tell you about existing travel warnings.

Green Cards: These are documents the U.S. Department of State has issued to foreign passport holders seeking residence in the U.S. They must be carried at all times.

FIGURE 1.1

STEP 1: The Travelers

LEGAL NAME OF PEOPLE TRAVELING:

Indicate LEGAL name and ages as discounts may apply. Be sure to add your name to list.

Name ______________________ Age ________

Name ______________________ Age ________

Name ______________________ Age ________

Name ______________________ Age ________

Name ______________________ Age ________

Name ______________________ Age ________

Memberships: AAA # ______________________

CHECK OFF WHEN COMPLETED

- ❑ Checked with each person to see if dates work
- ❑ Checked with each person for any objections
- ❑ Checked all work schedules
- ❑ Gotten permission for time off from work
- ❑ Checked the most current school vacation schedule
- ❑ Set up coverage at work
- ❑ Arranged dog walker, housesitter, caregiver, etc

FREQUENT FLYER INFORMATION

Note the number for the airline you prefer to use.

Airline ________________ Number______________

Airline ________________ Number______________

Airline ________________ Number______________

Airline ________________ Number______________

Airline ________________ Number______________

Airline ________________ Number______________

AARP #______________________________

OTHER PERTINENT INFORMATION:

- ❑ Does anyone have a disability that needs assistance?
  If so, whom ______________________________
  and what kind ____________________________.
- ❑ If traveling with a pet have you verified with airline?
- ❑ Do you have a government issued picture ID?

CHAPTER 2

Preplanning Step 2: The Importance of Timing

There is no other component of travel planning that is more important than THE DATE WHEN YOU BOOK YOUR TRIP. It can make the difference between confirming the plans you want at a price you can afford, and buying a very over-priced trip that doesn't really suit your needs.

You must also add in the time you spend doing research. The average vacation takes approximately one month to arrange. This depends on how much information you want to gather; and, if you are a detail-oriented researcher like me, this could be several more months! I need to have as much information in my hand as reasonably possible so I can feel comfortable about the decisions I need to make. I like to feel prepared. Whether I have all the information is unknown, but at least I feel good about it. Planning a vacation takes on many elements based on emotions. I need to feel

good about the planning part, just as much as the actual trip. The planning is a true part of the journey.

When Do You Want to Go?

Get out Your Calendars: The first thing you need to do is get out your calendars—both your personal and work calendars. And if you are traveling with children, get out their school and activities calendars. Also, check with your traveling companion(s) for their personal and work schedules.

FOR EXAMPLE: A family of 4: mom, dad and two children, ages 8 and 11, wants to take a winter vacation to Orlando. Obviously, the dates will have to be based on school vacations.

They have come to these conclusions:

- The family is not flexible on the week of travel
- It must be a school vacation week
- First choice of dates: February 14 to 23
- They can go for 7 to 10 days
- Got hubby's work calendar blocked
- Back-up date: Easter vacation week

You need to be this specific when attempting to confirm a trip to a warm climate during school vacation week.

How Long Will You Be Away?

This question was answered above as February 14 to 23. But, if you have only picked the relative week, you need to decide how many days you want to be away.

- Is it over the holiday weekend? How many days?
- Are you taking a long weekend? If so, which days?
- Are you going midweek?
- Are you traveling Saturday to Saturday?
- Are you traveling Friday to Sunday?
- Are you traveling 9 days or more?
- Are you retired? Can you travel at any time?

If you plan to travel midweek, Sunday through Friday, you will be paying considerably more for your airfare. Most discounted/nonrefundable "use it or lose it" airfares require you to stay over a Saturday night to qualify. Cities such as Las Vegas and Orlando have airfare rules that differ from the regular nonrefundable rules and offer some flexibility. Traveling to, or via, these two cities can bypass the Saturday night stay requirement for most fares.

- If you plan on traveling on a holiday weekend, or a "long weekend," how many days is this? It varies by person.
- Do you want to leave on Thursday night after work—6:00 P.M., or later? Or will you get up early on Friday morning and leave, at 7:00 A.M. (and avoid that extra hotel night)? Both require taking Friday off from work.
- Did you ask for the day off yet? Make a reservation, if possible, but do not pay for the ticket before asking for time off.
- Maybe you can only leave Friday night after work, around 6:00 P.M., and return on Monday night, the holiday, also around 6:00 P.M.

Timing Affects Where You Can Go

The flight schedules and flying time are key factors in determining the destination to which you can travel. There are rarely evening flights to the Caribbean, so Thursday night after 6:00 P.M. is not a possibility for most destinations, except San Juan. You could fly to Miami, stay overnight, or another Florida city that has an early morning flight to your island in the Caribbean. Keep in mind that you will have to pay for the hotel at the Florida airport.

FOR EXAMPLE: To fly New York City/Kennedy to Aruba on American Airlines takes 4½ hours. You have checked in at the airport at 8:30 A.M., 2 hours prior the 10:30 A.M. scheduled departure time and arrive approximately at 3:00 P.M. (In winter there is a one-hour time change that adds an hour to the total time.) Assume your flight is on time. After you collect your bags, you will go through customs and probably arrive at your hotel in time for dinner and not much else (a late swim, maybe). You have just lost one day of your "4 day" weekend.

On your last day, the return American Airlines flight leaves at 4:15 P.M. (5:15 P.M. with the winter time change). But flight check-in is 2 hours prior, at 2:15 P.M. Checkout time at the hotel is probably around 11:00 A.M. You store your bags, have a last swim and change your clothes in the public bathroom near the pool, all before a substantial late lunch around 12:30 P.M. You nervously await your ride to the airport. You check in for your flight and hang around waiting for your departure. This is another wasted day of your 4-day weekend. So in effect, your 4-day weekend has become a 2-day weekend with 2 full days of travel. DO YOU REALLY WANT TO GO THIS FAR FOR 2 DAYS AT THE BEACH?

No matter what dates you chose, Murphy's Law is in charge and something may go wrong to gum up your plans. You may not be booking far enough in advance or your choices may be sold out. A very common occurrence for the February long weekend is snow, lots of the white powdery stuff. If it snows and your flight does not get off the ground that day, you may spend your weekend sleeping on the floor in the airport. Your 4-day weekend has just been cancelled and you lose your full prepayment. (If you purchased trip cancellation insurance, it only covers weather if your airline has cancelled all flights to your destination for 48 hours.)

One last note for a 4-day weekend: you want to choose a destination that has several flights a day, not one that has one nonstop a day and few alternatives. Try to avoid connecting through cities that get an abundance of snowfall, especially Denver or Chicago/O'Hare, if you are going to a warm climate in winter.

When Should You Make Your Reservations?

This is difficult to answer. There are many different spins on this subject. Here are some choices; you decide. Once you have completed the *PRE-PLANNING STEPS* and feel you have done the necessary research, you may be ready to confirm and pay for your trip. See the air, hotel and car sections for booking information. Here are some points to keep in mind:

- Generally you should book your trip 30 to 60 days prior to your departure date to take advantage of the lowest nonrefundable fares.
- Watch the media for advertisements on airfare sales. (See explanation of "airfare sales" or "fare wars" in the section on airfare discounts.)

- Book your winter Florida vacation in July; watch for sales starting the last week of June. Buy your ticket before the summer sales end, usually mid-August. Again, see section on airfare discounts. If you missed the summer sale, start checking in mid-October for winter sales.
- Book your spring European vacation during the winter sales, usually from December to March.
- Book your summer European or other international vacation by the end of March. There may or may not be a sale, but if you wait any longer, the cheaper seats may have already sold out.
- If you are booking last minute, check out the "no frills" airlines for better fares, or check last-minute websites like *site59.com* for web deals.
- If you miss the airfare sales, try booking with a consolidator (see sources of airfare discounts for explanation.) for international or a travel bidding website like *Priceline.com* or *Expedia.com*'s Flight Price Matcher for domestic.
- If traveling over a school vacation, book your airline reservations 11 months in advance. This is the date, 330 days in advance, that airline flight schedules are added to the computer systems. Call at 12:01 A.M. and sit on hold till you reach someone. Or go online and book it. If you wait till 9:00 A.M. of that morning, the flight you want could be sold out. If you book by phone, you should have 24 hours to pay for your tickets. Booking online usually requires immediate purchase. Make sure you've done all your preplanning steps and research first. See the chapter, *Surf the Web for Airfares* for the best way to book an airline ticket. Once you have made your airline reservation, then you can book your hotel by securing it with either a deposit against your credit card or a full prepayment. Most resort destinations, especially at peak travel times—school vacations—usually require a deposit. See the hotel section for finding discounts, confirming and securing rooms with a deposit, and cancellation information.

STEP 2: When Do You Want to Go?

FIGURE 2.1

Date ____________

Is everyone in your party traveling the entire trip together? If not, use the "second choice" column for their dates and times.

FIRST CHOICE		SECOND CHOICE/SECOND GROUP	
People traveling	____________	Names	____________
	____________		____________
Departure date:	____________	Date	____________
Day of the week	____________	Day	____________
Depart at what time	____________	Time	____________
Return date:	____________	Date	____________
Day of the week	____________	Day	____________
Depart at what time	____________	Time	____________

The departure times are estimates. Actual departure times will depend on the flights you have chosen.

Elements that affect timing:

- How many miles from your home to the airport?
- How long does it take to get to airport from your home?
- How long does it take to get to your hotel?
- Do you have a tight schedule? Do you have a meeting scheduled?

CHAPTER 3

Preplanning Step 3: What Do You Want to Do on Vacation?

Another part of developing guidelines for your vacation is deciding what you want to do once you arrive. Choosing an island in the Caribbean may not be a good decision if you don't enjoy the sun or sand, and would rather be wandering around an art museum. If you are active night people and love bar-hopping an island also may not work. This is why you need to decide ahead of time what you want to do and then research destinations to see if they have what you want.

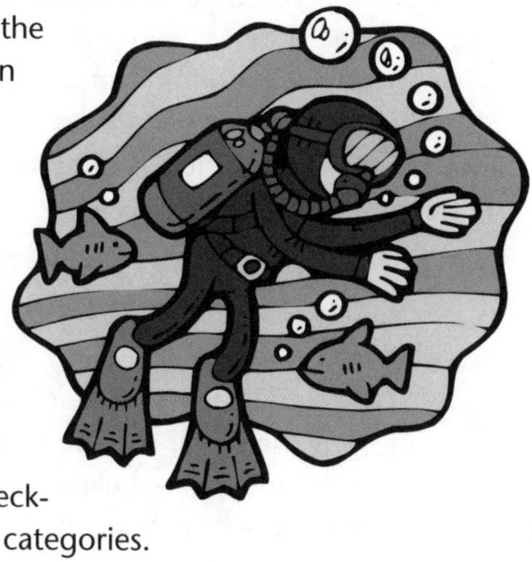

At the end of this chapter is a checklist of activities, broken down into categories.

Check off what you WANT to do on vacation, not necessarily what you do at home. Sometimes these activities overlap, sometimes not. This step is to focus you on activities that may need prearranging.

Also keep in mind what your travel companions want to do. Do both you and your companion want to play golf every day? Or is your hubby a golfer and you like the spa? You would want to pick out a resort that offers both. What about the kids? Do you want a children's program to keep them occupied while you are in the spa or playing golf? All activities should be considered when choosing a hotel or destination and are part of your research.

A VERY IMPORTANT NOTE: few people change their habits while on vacation. Thinking you will enjoy a week hiking in the mountains might not be realistic if the only walking you do is from your parked car to the store.

Need vs. Desires

Need: A need is the absolute minimum you are willing to accept for your vacation, e.g. an airline seat, a car, and a hotel room.

Desire/Want: A desire or want is anything more than just a need and costs more. You want a first-class seat or to travel on a heavily booked date; you want an SUV instead of taking the bus; or you want an ocean view room instead of a garden view room. *You will have to pay extra money to fulfill your desires.* Can you afford it and are you willing to pay extra?

Separating your needs from your desires is an exercise in indulgence and financial planning. The best way to do this is to first check your budget.

- If you have lots of money in the bank, you need to decide how much you are willing to spend to indulge in your desires.
- If you have limited extra income, are you financing your trip on your credit cards? What is the interest rate and how long will it take to pay them off? Do you care? Do you have enough credit to take care of unexpected expenses?
- Is there a reason why you should spend the extra money? A special occasion like a honeymoon or anniversary?

- Do you really need it? If you only sleep and shower in your hotel room can't you do that in a standard room instead of the most expensive suite?
- Are you planning your trip too late and all the cheap seats are sold out? Can you change your dates or fly to a different city?
- Will you use it? Buying a prepaid package that includes lots of sightseeing or meals may not be a good value if you don't want to go sightseeing every day or if you don't eat very much.

There are many things that may tempt you while planning your trip. Be realistic and ONLY BUY IN ADVANCE THOSE ITEMS YOU WILL REALLY USE, such as the airline ticket, transportation to your hotel, and a hotel room. It might seem like a bargain to buy a package trip that includes sightseeing or other items. It ceases to be a bargain if you do not use everything you have purchased. Rarely can you get your money back from the tour operator for components you do not use. On occasion you can save money by buying a prepaid package. It is mostly a convenience for your financial planning. You can always buy the theatre ticket or rent a golf cart, as you need them. Celebrity tours or other events that may sell out by the time you arrive should be purchased in advance.

FIGURE 3.1

STEP 3: What Do You Want to Do There?

- Does everyone want to do the same thing?
- How active are you at home? See below to decide.
- Do you want to do the same thing on vacation as you do at home?
- Do you want to do something different while on vacation?

WHAT DO YOU WANT TO DO ON VACATION:

Check off those that apply. If someone wants to do something different, put his initials on the line. Mark important Must Do activities with an asterisk.

Daytime Activities:

_____ sightseeing
_____ lay on beach
_____ museum
_____ city tour
_____ walk on beach
_____ historic sites
_____ shopping
_____ sleeping
_____ historic tours
_____ gambling
_____ relax
_____ lectures
_____ visit family

_____ symphony
_____ bar hopping
_____ rock concert
_____ concert
_____ partying
_____ nightclubs
_____ soiree
_____ dinner theatre
_____ shopping
other ______________
other ______________

Special Events:

_____ sporting event
_____ convention
_____ celebrity show
_____ Super Bowl
_____ World Series

HOW ACTIVE A PERSON ARE YOU? AND YOUR TRAVELING COMPANIONS?

Low Activity

_____ couch potato
_____ sits at a desk all day

______ swim
______ zoo
______ visit friends
______ walks
______ wander
______ driving
______ water park
______ adventure prk
______ reading
______ working
______ spa, massage
other ______________
other ______________

Evening Activities:
______ dining
______ gambling
______ theater
______ dancing
______ walk
______ opera
______ drinking
______ celebrity show

Sports:
______ tennis
______ golf
______ snow ski
______ swim
______ water sports
______ water ski
______ lay on beach
______ beach sports
______ sailing
______ hiking
______ biking
______ mountain climb
______ long walks
______ dance
______ racing
______ run, jog
______ gym workout
other ______________
other ______________

______ drives everywhere
______ video games
______ internet surfer
______ watches a lot of TV
______ watches sports

Moderate Activity:
______ house cleaning
______ walk to shopping
______ yard work

High Activity:
______ exercises daily
______ goes to gym
______ long walks
______ hiking
______ biking
______ roller blading
______ takes part in sports

CHAPTER 4

Preplanning Step 4: Where Do You Want to Go?

What Affects Where You Can Go:

- Time of year
- Length of trip
- Climate
- Availability of flights
- School vacation period
- Holiday migration
- Long holiday weekend
- Political situation
- Family
- What you want to do on vacation

When you want to go and *for how long* has a direct correlation to *where* you can go. If you want to travel over a long holiday weekend, 3 to 4 days, you want to pick a destination that is not too far away, where the flying time is under 3 hours, and the flights leave at times convenient to your schedule. See Chapter 2 for details on time guidelines.

Most family travel is during school vacation. If you are traveling to a popular family destination such as a ski destination, the Caribbean, Mexico, Florida or Hawaii, you need to plan these trips as far in advance as possible to get confirmation of hotel space, airline tickets and car rentals. These sell out almost a year in advance over peak holidays such as Christmas, February/winter school break, and Easter. Also, keep in mind that discounts are rarely offered for peak time periods. It's the old supply and demand rule: the more demand for a product with a limited supply, the higher they charge for it. This is especially true for hotels. Airline discounts can be had if booked 11 months in advance at midnight. But the deeply discounted fares are usually "blacked out"—not offered for sale on these heavily in demand dates.

If you live in a cold climate, the warm destinations and flights between them sell out quickly, as do the hotels. The same goes for ski destinations. When there is great demand for a product, heavy restrictions are usually attached to them so they can maximize usage and revenue. Hotels usually require large deposits or full prepayment. Deposit may be required to confirm the reservation, and no refund of this hefty deposit is possible. Some cancellation policies require 45 to 60 days in advance. It is essential that you ask about the cancellation policy before giving your credit card number. If you are in any way unsure as to whether you are going, do not make any payment until you are sure, or you may lose it.

If you hear on the news that a country is having political problems or bad weather, it would make sense not to visit there at the moment. The U.S. government has a website for travel warnings and advisories. Check this out before you plan a trip to that destination:

http://travel.state.gov/travel_warnings.html.

Tips to Help You Decide Where to Go:

- Ask a friend with similar interests where they've been lately.
- Watch the Travel Channel for ideas.
- Rent travel videos from the library or video store.
- Visit the travel section of a library or bookstore.
- Scan travel magazines.

- Surf the web.
- Speak to a vacation-oriented travel agent.
- Throw a dart at a map on the wall.

When you ask friends about their favorite trip, keep in mind that their trip was planned with their parameters and not yours. If they are tennis buffs and you are not, the resort they stayed at may not be quite right for you. Ask them what they liked about the destination and what they disliked. Use this as a guideline.

If you are not sure where you would like to go, find travel guides about the general area you would like to visit, i.e., the Caribbean, ski destinations, or Europe. If you have a lot of free time, go online and research the destination you have in mind.

If you have specific activities that you want to do, i.e., play tennis, golf or ski, you should have a general idea of where you can go. If you need help focusing on activities, look over the activities sheet (Figure 3.1) in Chapter 3: "WHAT DO YOU WANT TO DO THERE?"

FOR EXAMPLE: Ethel has decided that her family wants to play, get some exercise and relax. She's leaning toward a destination that has an amusement park, warm climate and shopping. She could either go to Orlando, home of Walt Disney World, Sea World and Universal Studios in Florida, or the Disneyland area in California. She has researched both destinations and has found the cost for a vacation in Florida is far cheaper than California. Always budget conscious, Orlando and Disney World was her choice.

Her neighbor, Alice, decided her husband Ralph was not the active type and decided on an inexpensive beach holiday in the Bahamas. They could hang out at the pool, walk along the beach, and pig out at the buffets.

Tips on Selecting a Destination

- Make a list of people going, with ages.
- Note any hobbies: roller blading, fishing, etc.
- List where you've been before, what you did there, and did everyone enjoy it? Would you like to go back there or try something different?
- Make a list of what activities you would like to do on this trip. Are they realistic or fantasy? Number them in order of "must do" to "maybe."

- Time of year.
- Length of vacation.
- List possible destinations.
- Research each destination to see if they have the activities you most want to do.
- Research flying time and flight schedules.
- Research air fare availability.
- Research hotels: What activities do they have to offer? Do they have rooms available? What are the rates?
- Discuss with travel partners and make a choice.

Step 4: How to Determine Where to Go

See Figure 4.1. This fill-in sheet is to assist you in narrowing down your research choices. First, you need to look at your time guidelines. Are you traveling over a school break or holiday time period when availability is limited and more expensive? If so, then make a list of activities or hobbies you would like to do on vacation. People tend to maintain the same activity level on vacation as they do at home. If you are a couch potato, you most likely won't enjoy hiking while on vacation. Make a note of places you have traveled to in the past. Did you like it? Do you want to go back? Or do you want to do something different this trip? List destinations you are interested in and then research each one. Sometimes the availability and flying time will rule out a particular destination.

STEP 4: How to Determine Where to Go

FIGURE 4.1

1. Timing: When do you want to go? Are your dates over a school break or holiday vacation?

   Dates ______________________ Number of days ______________________

2. List the hobbies and activities that you would like to do. Does everyone want to participate?

3. Where have you traveled to before? What did you like about it? What did you dislike about it? Would you return there?

4. Do you want something new? ❑ YES ❑ NO

5. List possibilities to research:

CHAPTER 5

Preplanning Step 5: Budget and Payments

How much can you afford to spend on this trip? Will you be paying by check or putting everything on one or more credit cards? Will you pay off the entire credit card at once or stretch the payments over 6 months? It is difficult to determine in advance exactly how much a trip will cost. Even prepaying an all-inclusive vacation has added costs you may not expect.

Tips to Keep Your Costs Under Control:

- When prepaying any component of your trip, ask what is included in the prepaid rate. Write it down on the TRIP ESTIMATES SHEET (Figure 5.2) at the end of chapter.
- Be sure to get in writing what you have actually paid for.
- Ask what other charges you may be expected to pay, i.e., taxes, service charges, tipping, departure taxes.
- Ask about the cancellation policy, and any miscellaneous fees if you check out early or fly home on a different date.
- Determine whether or not you really need that deluxe ocean view room. See Chapter 3, *Needs vs. Desires.*

Do you have any idea what your trip will cost? Have you done any research: called the airlines, looked on-line, spoken to a travel agent? You need to have a clear idea of what a trip will cost before you give your credit card number as payment. Postpone your decision to buy until you have some idea of the cost of your trip. Then you can avoid any surprises that may blow you off budget.

How Will You Pay for Your Trip?

The most common way to pay for your trip is by credit card. If you do not have a credit card, try to get one. There are several reasons why you want to pay by credit card instead of cash or check.

- ***The first, and most important, reason to use a credit card is for your financial protection.***

If you were to pay by cash or check and the company goes out of business or takes your money and does not pay for your product, you are out of luck. You could sue them, but few people are willing to bother with the involved hassles of suing. (And you still won't be going on that planned trip.) If you chose to pay by check or cash, understand that you have increased your liability and could lose what you have paid. For your protection, get a receipt with the amount, date of travel, what the payment is for, and a legible signature. It would make sense to only give cash or a check to someone you know personally or who has an established reputation in your area. There are no guarantees that even this will protect you, as people's ethics and business circumstances can change. Greed is a powerful motivator.

Also, in the horrific age of terrorism:

- ***Tickets that are not paid for by a credit card are singled out at the security checkpoint.***

You could be subject to additional questioning and/or possibly a body search by the security staff.

Another reason you want to use a credit card is:

- ***They are the payment method required by most travel related vendors.***

You cannot rent a car without one. Yes, you can pay by cash when you return your car, but the car rental company still requires that you have a credit card in your name to rent. Also, you must have a certain amount of available credit on that card. Some companies actually block your credit card for a specific amount, possibly double the contracted rate. Ask at the counter if they do this, and the amount that they will block. The car companies judge your financial integrity by the owning of a credit card.

- ***Most hotels will not confirm a reservation unless you give them a credit card number as a "guarantee."***

If you don't show up, they have your agreement to charge your credit card. The "terms" of confirming a reservation include this guarantee and billing policy.

- ***Airlines and travel agents require a credit card to purchase a ticket online or by phone. (Travel agents also require picture identification).***

When you buy an airline ticket online, you are required to enter a credit card number at the time of booking. If you make a reservation with an airline by telephone and want to pay by check, they will send you an invoice prior to issuing your ticket. Few airlines still allow you to pay this way. This would have to be done far enough in advance for your check to clear your bank and you to satisfy the airfare's advance purchase requirements.

A Word about Credit Cards

If an airline goes bankrupt or out of business and you have purchased your ticket *within 60 days of departure,* you can "dispute" the charge with your credit card company and ask for a refund. Call your credit card company and ask them how you dispute a charge for a bankrupt airline or travel vendor and what the rules and limitations are. You will probably have to do this in writing within 60 days of the charge.

Be sure to call your credit card company and ask them about their refund policy if a company goes out of business. You might have to push to get the information by asking for a supervisor. The card companies reluctantly release this information.

Fraudulent Use of Credit Cards

If you are one of those folks who prefers to use someone else's credit card for your airline tickets—BE WARNED: The airlines are no longer carrying the

AUTHOR'S NOTE

If you fly an airline with a fuzzy financial picture, you would be best served if you purchased your airline ticket no more than 60 days in advance. Otherwise you could possibly lose your money. If you travel on a school or holiday vacation when airline seats are at a premium, buy as soon as you can get them. Keep in mind your liability if the airline goes bankrupt.

financial burden. They can tell if the credit card number used does not belong to the traveler and WILL catch you at the airport when you check in. (Remember that government picture identification you need for check in?) You might spend your vacation in a jail cell instead of that beachfront resort!!

Those Hidden Charges

Throughout the travel industry there are numerous ways to separate you from your hard-earned dollar. Advertising prices may look attractive until you get the REAL price when you confirm. My favorite is the advertising of airline tickets. Every ad I have seen has advertised the price of an airline ticket without the added surcharges. The price advertised is the tariff BASE FARE that has a MANDATORY COLLECTION of numerous "taxes." Some could add $100 or more to the price of your ticket. This information is in tiny print at the bottom of the ad or spoken by some speed talker on the radio. This is deceptive advertising and "they" get away with it.

Airline Tickets: Normally when you purchase an airline ticket, you have prepaid most of the taxes and fees. There are occasionally additional taxes and fees on domestic tickets that may not have been collected at the time of purchase. A good example is the adding of fuel surcharges to airline tickets. This extra charge is handled differently among the airlines. One will collect in advance $20 per segment or flight. Another may not collect it at all, or only collect it in advance for specific markets and specific fares. Rarely will an airline collect a fee such as this from a passenger after the ticket has been issued.

Internationally it is a different story. Most countries charge a tax for exiting their country, called a departure tax. Unless that country has made an agreement with the specific airline to collect the departure tax in advance, you will have to pay this tax in CASH (preferably in local currency) at check-in. Usually is it under USD40, but ask your travel agent or airline what the fee is. (No one has ever asked me this question!) Many travel guides list the departure taxes and any other fees that may be collected by an airline at check-in.

Car Rentals: are getting ridiculous with their additional charges. Be sure to ask the agent who has confirmed your car reservation to give you a list of all the taxes and fees that are additional. (Or if booking online, check with the individual car company's website.) This could add another 40 percent to the cost of your car rental rate. For example, some additional charges at the Orlando airport may include:

- 9.8% for airport access (that bus you took)
- 6% state sales tax
- $2.05 per day Florida surcharge/tire fee
- 40¢ per day vehicle license recovery fee
- 3¢ per day recycling fee recovery
- 7.5% frequent flyer excise tax—fee to get your frequent flyer points (and you thought they came free!)
- Plus any insurance you may need. See car chapter.

My all-time favorite surcharge city is Boston. Some brilliant politician decided to get the tourists and visiting businessmen to finance a new convention center and has tacked on a $10 fee to any car rental to pay for it! There is also a 30¢ parking fine recovery fee, along with the 21% for the vehicle's registration, bus/concession fee and tax. The only thing you can do is to write a protest letter to your congressman. These additional charges are under investigation by the government.

Hotels: These folks have become very inventive in what they think they can tack on to your hotel bill. You should ask at check-in what kind of surcharges they add to your bill and what specific freebee you are actually paying for. See hotel chapter. That free newspaper and access to the gym may be added to your bill at checkout whether or not you read the paper or used the gym.

Case in point: Once, at the "Pretty" Hotel in Las Vegas, (fictitious name), I was given a "free" coupon booklet that included a casino chip and a free meal. At checkout, I discovered I was charged $50 for this "free" item. They said they would gladly refund the charge if I returned the booklet. They also knew that I had redeemed the coupons and was unable to return the booklet. I was never told there was a fee for this "free coupon booklet." The year before, I stayed there at the same time of year and received a similar "free coupon booklet." It was truly free then, so I assumed it to be the second time. I protested at checkout and no one at the front desk—clerk, front desk manager or hotel manager, would help me. They chose to ignore me. (Could this lousy customer service be a reason why the big hotel chain no longer manages them?) I had to pay the $50 for the "free coupon booklet." This seemed like a SCAM to me at the time. Las Vegas is filled with misinformation, so be very careful when booking and prepaying. Only give your credit card to a trusted source and get in writing the confirmation, per night rate, what is included, location of room, and cancellation policy.

Step 5: Budgeting Fill-in Sheet

See Figure 5.1, How will you pay for your trip? This form is self-explanatory. Will you pay by cash, check or credit card? If you will pay by cash or check, see the section above about your lack of financial protection. If you are using more than one credit card, fill in the section that says, "Use this credit card for__________." Some people charge the hotel to one card, and the airline tickets to another credit card. Indicating on this sheet what you are charging to which credit card will make it easier in the end to keep track of your expenses. See the TRIP ESTIMATES sheet for tracking.

Trip Estimates

See Figure 5.2. To stay within your budget, it is always a good idea to make a list of potential expenses. The TRIP ESTIMATES fill-in sheet lists each major component of your trip, airfare, car rental, hotels, meals and activities, along with estimated taxes and fees.

In the Notes section at the bottom, you may want to list activities that you want to do, i.e., movies, etc. but will not prepay.

Tips to Save Money

- Cut down on the number of days you will be away. If your original plan is to stay 10 days, compare the total price for 7, 8 or 9 days.
- Change your departure date. Midweek travel can be cheaper.
- Stay over a Saturday night to get a cheaper airfare.
- Check the hotel for lower rates on different check-in dates. A midweek rate at a business hotel may be more expensive than a Friday or Saturday arrival.
- Downgrade your room, i.e., switch from an ocean view to a mountain view.
- Also see the specific sections on airfare, hotel and car discounts.
- Use ATM machines for cash as needed instead of travelers checks. See: *www.visa.com/atms* for locations. Have money in your checking account, as some international bank ATMs cannot access savings accounts. Also, 4-digit pin numbers are the norm.

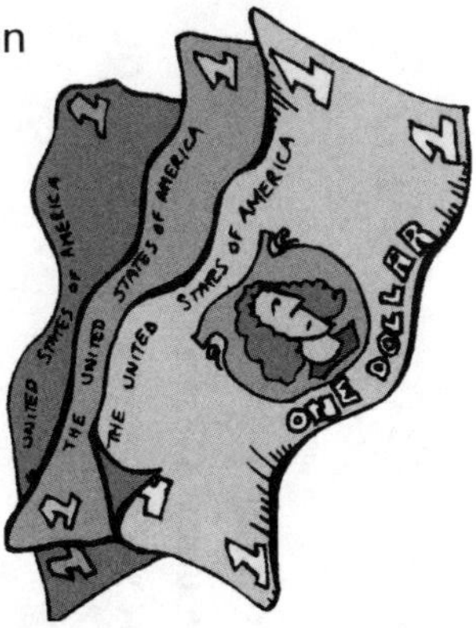

- Use a credit card whenever possible. It is safer than carrying a lot of cash, and you get a better exchange rate than using travelers checks.

Points to Note

- Ask what is included in the prepaid rate. Get a written confirmation stating exactly what you have reserved and prepaid.
- When booking your car rental, ask what taxes and fees will be added to your final bill. When you pick up your car, ask to have the extra charges circled on your contract. When you use the car rental company's express service, ask for a copy of the contract at the exit gate where they check for your license.
- When confirming your hotel, ask what additional charges may be added to your bill, especially the usually excessive telephone and computer charges. If breakfast is included, get some kind of slip to present to the waiter.
- Verify cancellation policy on all reservations.

STEP 5: How Will You Pay for Your Trip?

FIGURE 5.1

How will you be paying for your trip? ❑ Check ❑ Cash (Neither method recommended)

PLEASE NOTE: If you are paying by check or cash, you are at an increased risk of losing your money if the company goes bankrupt, or may be singled out at the airport for extensive security search. Use your credit card if possible.

❑ Credit card: ❑ AMEX ❑ DINERS CLUB ❑ DISCOVER ❑ VISA ❑ MASTER CARD ❑ Other ______

1st card name/number ______ Exp. date ______

Name as it appears on credit card: ______

Address on the credit card statement: ______

______

Preprinted codes ______

Use this card for: ❑ airline tickets ❑ hotel #1 ❑ hotel #2 ❑ car ❑ other ______

❑ Credit card: ❑ AMEX ❑ DINERS CLUB ❑ DISCOVER ❑ VISA ❑ MASTER CARD ❑ Other ______

2nd card name/number ______ Exp. date ______

Name as it appears on credit card: ______

Address on the credit card statement: ______

______

Preprinted codes ______

Use this card for: ❑ airline tickets ❑ hotel #1 ❑ hotel #2 ❑ car ❑ other ______

Trip Estimates

FIGURE 5.2

Date ____________________

TOTALS

AIRLINE TICKETS:

fare per adult __________ x number of adults ________ = total ________________

fare per child __________ x number of children ______ = total ________________

other airfares __________ x number of others ________ = total ________________

TOTAL ESTIMATE ________________

Charged to credit card # ______________________________________ exp date ____________

GROUND TRANSPORTATION AT DESTINATION: (not car rental)

❑ Someone picking you up ❑ airport bus ❑ taxi ❑ limousine

rate per adult _______ x _________ = total ________________

rate per child _______ x _________ = total ________________

other rate _______ x _________ = total ________________

PREPAID: ❑ YES ❑ NO **TOTAL ESTIMATE** ________________

Charged to credit card # ______________________________________ exp date ____________

or

CAR RENTAL: **CAR COMPANY**________________

Is base rate a: ❑ daily ❑ weekly ❑ weekend ❑ other: ____________________

Base rate $_________ x number of days/weeks _______ = total ________________

PLUS: state tax _____% ________________________

local tax _____% ________________________

misc. fee _____% ________________________

misc. fee _____% ________________________

insurance/type ______ x days________ = ________________

gasoline ________________________

parking/daily _______ x days________ = ________________

BASE RATE PREPAID: ❑ YES ❑ NO

TOTAL ESTIMATE ________________

Charged to credit card # ______________________________________ exp date ____________

HOTEL #1: Name ______________________________________ dates ________________

base rate: city ________________

nightly, date: ______ @ __________ x nts ______ = total ________________

nightly, date: ______ @ __________ x nts ______ = total ________________

weekly, dates: ______ @ __________ x nts ______ = total ________________

other, dates: ______ @ __________ x nts ______ = total ________________

state tax ______ % = total ________________

local tax ______ % = total ________________

misc. fee ______ % for ____________ = total ________________

misc. fee ______ % for ____________ = total ________________

PREPAID AMOUNT: ________________ includes: ________________________________

TOTAL ESTIMATE ________________

Charged to credit card # ______________________________________ exp date ____________

HOTEL #2: Name ______________________________ dates ______________
base rate: city ______________
nightly, date: ______ @ __________ x nts ______ = total ______________
nightly, date: ______ @ __________ x nts ______ = total ______________
weekly, dates: ______ @ __________ x nts ______ = total ______________
other, dates: ______ @ __________ x nts ______ = total ______________
state tax ______ % = total ______________
local tax ______ % = total ______________
misc. fee ______ % for __________ = total ______________
misc. fee ______ % for __________ = total ______________
PREPAID AMOUNT: ______________ includes: ______________________________
TOTAL ESTIMATE ______________
Charged to credit card # ______________________________ exp date __________

HOTEL #3: Name ______________________________ dates ______________
base rate: city ______________
nightly, date: ______ @ __________ x nts ______ = total ______________
nightly, date: ______ @ __________ x nts ______ = total ______________
weekly, dates: ______ @ __________ x nts ______ = total ______________
other, dates: ______ @ __________ x nts ______ = total ______________
state tax ______ % = total ______________
local tax ______ % = total ______________
misc. fee ______ % for __________ = total ______________
misc. fee ______ % for __________ = total ______________
PREPAID AMOUNT: ______________ includes: ______________________________
TOTAL ESTIMATE ______________
Charged to credit card # ______________________________ exp date __________

HOTEL #4/OTHER: Name ______________________________ dates ______________
base rate: city ______________
nightly, date: ______ @ __________ x nts ______ = total ______________
nightly, date: ______ @ __________ x nts ______ = total ______________
weekly, dates: ______ @ __________ x nts ______ = total ______________
other, dates: ______ @ __________ x nts ______ = total ______________
state tax ______ % = total ______________
local tax ______ % = total ______________
misc. fee ______ % for __________ = total ______________
misc. fee ______ % for __________ = total ______________
PREPAID AMOUNT: ______________ includes: ______________________________
TOTAL ESTIMATE ______________
Charged to credit card # ______________________________ exp date __________

ACTIVITIES:
TYPE OF PASS/LIFT TKT, ETC. ______________________________
Dates: ________ adults each @ __________ x ______ = ______________
Dates: ________ children ea. @ __________ x ______ = ______________
other ____________ each @ __________ x ______ = ______________
TOTAL ESTIMATE ______________
Charged to credit card # ______________________________ exp date __________

MEALS:

BREAKFAST:	$__________ x adults	______ x days ______	= total	________________
	$__________ x chd	______ x days ______	= total	________________
LUNCH:	$__________ x adults	______ x days ______	= total	________________
	$__________ x chd	______ x days ______	= total	________________
DINNER:	$__________ x adults	______ x days ______	= total	________________
	$__________ x chd	______ x days ______	= total	________________
SPECIAL EVENT:	$__________ x adults	______ x days ______	= total	________________
	$__________ x chd	______ x days ______	= total	________________

PREPAID: ❑ YES ❑ NO

TOTAL ESTIMATE ____________________

GROUND TRANSPORTATION RETURN DATE:

❑ someone driving you ❑ Car rental: see above section

❑ airport bus:

rate per adult _____________ x __________ = total ________________

rate per child _____________ x __________ = total ________________

special rate _____________ x __________ = total ________________

❑ taxi ❑ limousine ❑ estimated tip __________ = total ________________

❑ other, specify________________________________ = total ________________

TOTAL ESTIMATE ____________________

Charged to credit card # ____________________________________ exp date ____________

ESTIMATE TOTAL

AIRLINE TICKETS:	Used credit card #	______________________________________
CAR RENTAL #1:	Used credit card #	______________________________________
CAR RENTAL #2:	Used credit card #	______________________________________
HOTEL #1:	Used credit card #	______________________________________
HOTEL #2:	Used credit card #	______________________________________
HOTEL #3:	Used credit card #	______________________________________
PASSES ETC.	Used credit card #	______________________________________
OTHER __________	Used credit card #	______________________________________
OTHER __________	Used credit card #	______________________________________

FINAL ESTIMATE TOTAL ______________

NOTES:

CHAPTER 6

Preplanning Step 6: How to Get There

If you have followed the preplanning steps, you have already:

- Decided who is going
- Defined your travel dates
- Decided what activities you will do there
- Chosen a destination
- Determined how much can you afford to spend.

Now you need to determine the best way to get there. Should you fly, drive, take a train, or travel by some other means of transportation?

Deciding whether to fly, drive, or take a train is a matter of preference, desired experience, and physical ability. If you have a fear of flying, you will find another way to travel. If you cannot sit for long periods of time in confined spaces, you may want to take a train that allows you to get up and walk around. If you have never taken a cruise, you might choose this as a new experience. (But you still need to determine how you'll reach the cruise ship.)

If you will fly, which airline should you take and into what airport? How long does the flight take? Are there nonstop flights or will you have to change plans enroute? And most importantly, are there any cheap seats available on your chosen dates? ***You need to research to find out the answers.*** See the chapters on the *Airline Route System* and the *Airline Hub and Spoke System* for background information on the best way to plan your trip by air.

If you will drive, do you have a map of the area? Do you know how long the drive will be? Do you need to plan stops along the way? Will you drive your own a car, or will you rent? See the chapter on car rentals for information.

If you have never taken a train, you are missing out on one glorious experience. It can be relaxing. You have lots of legroom and can walk around to your heart's content. If you are claustrophobic, you might be more comfortable on a train than on an airplane. AMTRAK, the U.S.'s train system, has wonderfully scenic areas throughout their system and is well worth the time and investment.

SUMMARY PART ONE: PREPLANNING

Before you pick up the phone or search online, you must have your guidelines ready. The preplanning steps gather this information onto fill-in sheets included in this book. These key steps are:

STEP 1: Who are you traveling with, names and ages
STEP 2: Timing, when do you want to go and for how long
STEP 3: What activities would you like to do there
STEP 4: Where do you want to go
STEP 5: Budget and payments, how much can you afford and how will you pay for it
STEP 6: How to get there: choose your mode of transportation.

The final fill-in sheet for Part 1 is the *SUMMARY PREPLANNING SHEET*. Take the information from the individual steps and put them on this sheet. When finished with this first part, go on to the research section then to the specific fill-in sheets for airline tickets and hotels. These sheets are in the relevant chapters, see contents for pages.

Preplanning Summary Sheet FIGURE 6.1

Group Coordinator: ______________________ Date __________________

STEP 1: LEGAL NAMES, AGES, FREQUENT FLYER NUMBER:

______________________ AGE _____ FREQ FLYER# __________________

______________________ AGE _____ FREQ FLYER# __________________

______________________ AGE _____ FREQ FLYER# __________________

MEMBERSHIPS: AAA #_________________ AARP # ____________________

STEP 2: TIMING: WHEN ARE YOU GOING?

	FIRST CHOICE		SECOND CHOICE
DEPARTURE DATE	____________	date	____________
Day of the week	____________	day	____________
Desired time	____________	time	____________
RETURN DATE	____________	date	____________
Day of the week	____________	day	____________
Desired time	____________	time	____________

STEP 3: WHAT DO YOU WANT TO DO THERE?

Is there a theme to your trip? Family reunion, tournament, or concert? List activities that need to be prearranged:

STEP 4: WHERE ARE YOU GOING?

DESTINATION:

STEP 5: HOW WILL YOU PAY FOR YOUR TRIP?

❑ Check ❑ Cash (Neither method recommended)

❑ Credit card: ❑ AMEX ❑ DINERS CLUB ❑ DISCOVER ❑ VISA ❑ MASTER CARD ❑ OTHER _____

1st card number ______________________________ exp.date___________

Name as it appears on credit card: ______________________________

Address on the credit card statement______________________________

Any preprinted codes _________________

Use this card for: ❑ airline tickets ❑ hotel #1 ❑ hotel #2 ❑ other __________

2nd card number ______________________________ exp.date___________

Name as it appears on credit card: ______________________________

Address on the credit card statement______________________________

Any preprinted codes _________________

Use this card for: ❑ airline tickets ❑ hotel #1 ❑ hotel #2 ❑ other __________

STEP 6: HOW TO GET THERE:

**Coordinate with information from the airline reservation sheet

Group Summary Sheet

FIGURE 6.2

STEP 1: NAMES AND AGES OF TRAVELERS:

____________________ AGE _____ FREQ FLYER# ____________________

____________________ AGE _____ FREQ FLYER# ____________________

____________________ AGE _____ FREQ FLYER# ____________________

____________________ AGE _____ FREQ FLYER# ____________________

____________________ AGE _____ FREQ FLYER# ____________________

MEMBERSHIPS:

AAA # ____________________ cardholder ____________________

AARP # ____________________ cardholder ____________________

Is everyone traveling together on ENTIRE trip? ❑ YES ❑ NO

**Use a separate sheet for people traveling at different times.

STEP 2: TIMING

	FIRST CHOICE		SECOND CHOICE
DEPARTURE DATE	__________	date	__________
Day of the week	__________	day	__________
Desired time	__________	time	__________
RETURN DATE	__________	date	__________
Day of the week	__________	day	__________
Desired time	__________	time	__________

STEP 3: WHAT DO YOU WANT TO DO THERE?

Is there a theme to your trip? Family reunion, golf tournament, concert? List your major reason for the trip and note what needs to be prearranged or prepaid.

STEP 4: WHERE ARE YOU GOING?

DESTINATION:

STEP 5: HOW WILL YOU PAY FOR YOUR TRIP? Ask each family group for a credit card to use for guaranteeing hotels, depending on booking source. DO NOT PURCHASE ANY TRAVEL ITEM FOR THEM.

Name__________________ Credit card # ____________________ exp. _____

Name__________________ Credit card # ____________________ exp. _____

Name__________________ Credit card # ____________________ exp. _____

SEE TRIP ESTIMATES FILL-IN SHEET FOR BUDGETING.

STEP 6: HOW WILL YOU GET THERE?

DEPARTURE AND DESTINATION CITIES/AIRPORTS

Which airport will you depart from? Where are you going? Keep in mind an alternate airport may offer discount airlines.

Departure city ______________________________

Departure airport: 1st _____________________ 2nd _______________________

Destination city ____________________________

Destination airport: 1st ____________________ 2nd _______________________

This form assumes you will fly. If you drive, take a train or bus note particulars here.

HOW WILL YOU BOOK YOUR TRIP?

❑ DON'T KNOW YET

❑ TRAVEL AGENT/Name________________ phone _________________________

❑ ONLINE/Source ____________________ URL address_____________________

❑ BY TELEPHONE/Number ____

Will you book each component separately or buy a prepaid, nonrefundable package?

❑ Separately ❑ Package ❑ Source: _________________________________

VARIOUS COMPONENTS OF YOUR TRIP:

AIRLINE RESEARCH:

Which airlines fly from your home airport to your destination?

GROUND TRANSPORTATION

❑ TRAIN ❑ BUS ❑ VAN ❑ LIMO ❑ CAR RENTAL

Number of vehicles needed ____________________

Name of driver (1) __________________ credit card _______________________

Name of driver (2) __________________ credit card _______________________

Preferred car rental company ____

I.D. number (1) ________________________ (2) ________________________

Size, make of car________________________ No. of people per car____________

Special features needed ____

HOTELS

NAME OF HOTEL #1 ________________________ phone number __________

Check-in date ____________________________ number of nights __________

Room #1 names ___________________________ number of beds __________

Room #2 names ___________________________ number of beds __________

NAME OF HOTEL #2 ________________________ phone number __________

Check-in date ____________________________ number of nights __________

Room #1 names ___________________________ number of beds __________

Room #2 names ___________________________ number of beds __________

Part Two: Gathering Information

Chapter 7 Research You Must Do 49

CHAPTER 7

Research You Must Do

One of the most important steps in planning a trip is the preliminary research. You have determined your guidelines but you are still unsure where you want to go. Doing general research can help you decide.

Review Your Guidelines

First review your guidelines set in the preplanning steps.

- WHO: name of people and ages
- WHEN: relative dates you have chosen
- WHAT: activities you will do
- WHERE: what destination
- HOW: which mode of transportation
- BUDGET: how much can you afford

How to Do Research

The type of research you must do varies according to your guidelines. A trip to Europe, visiting big cities and museums, is very different from a trip to the Caribbean. A trip than is not during school vacation will have different prices and availability (and be less crowded).

This is how I would approach my research:

Get Out My Calendar

This was done in Step 2 and now you're double-checking the dates. Do you have the most current school calendar? The time of year you plan on traveling and how far in advance you plan your trip has a dramatic influence on the outcome. Airline seat availability is difficult to predict. A quick call to a travel agent or possibly to the airline that serves your destination can give you an idea if the flights are heavily booked or sold out. See the chapter, *Understanding the Airline Route System*, for the best airline to call. American Airlines is always a good choice for the Caribbean, Delta for Orlando or Florida. Trying to determine this by searching online is a lot harder. You may only get a limited number of options based on your specific date and time input. A travel agent or an airline reservation agent looks at a screen with 6 flights and availability at once. When they see a screen full of zeros it's easy to determine that you'll have a difficult time finding a seat. And forget about getting a discount.

See the chapter, *Anatomy of an Airfare*, for a picture of the availability screen and sample explanation of airfares.

Gather Reference Material

- Computer with Internet for web surfing, if possible
- Travel guides
- Maps
- Hotel guides
- Tour brochures
- Telephone yellow pages
- Airline schedules
- List of airline phone numbers
- *Preplanning summary sheet* (Figure 6.1)
- Air and hotel sheets
- A blank notebook or pad
- Index cards (easy carry size)

This is a basic list of reference material. As you do your research, you will probably find other items to add to your collection. By the time I am ready to take my trip, I usually have a stack of travel guides, both purchased and borrowed from the library, an array of maps, brochures, and notes that I've collected and transferred to index cards. I sort through the index cards and take the ones I will need on my trip. They are usually cards listing restaurants, sights by area, and other handy reminders such as a shopping list.

Sources for Reference Material

- Internet
- Library
- Travel agency—ask for tour brochures
- Bookstore, travel section
- Tourist office, convention and visitors centers
- ***DISCOUNT TRAVEL WISDOM***

There are thousands of sites on the INTERNET that give you travel information. If you are overwhelmed by this task, go to a search engine such as *ask.com*. First, enter the name of the destination in the "search" box. Read through the list presented and then go to the bottom of the first page (sometimes it's at the top). There you will find drop-down boxes with questions such as, "where can I find tourist information for XXX (the name you typed in on the first screen) or "where can I find XXX about country XXX"? This program recognizes geographic names and places. This is a great place to start. Take notes as you surf. Note the website addresses or bookmark them on your browser. Use index cards to take notes.

If you do not own a computer or do not yet have access to the internet on yours, GO TO YOUR LOCAL LIBRARY and use one there. The library I use has 12 computers for the public to share. They have a sign-up sheet for each computer and allow each person 20-minute increments of blocked time. Visit yours and see what they have to offer.

While you're at the library, check out the travel section and search for books about your destination. I usually grab 5 or 6 books and head for a table to do my research. I scan each book's table of contents to see what's in the book and if it would be useful to me. Maps get my attention quickly. A good map can help travel planning immensely. Again, take notes on index cards.

This same principle works for BOOKSTORES. But you'll probably have to buy the book to take notes.

Next, call or visit the TOURIST OFFICE OR CONVENTION AND VISITORS CENTER. Many tourist board websites are filled with general information. Make notes on index cards instead of printing out numerous pages. I have found that the websites of various tourist boards are incomplete and have the bare minimum of information stored online. If you visit a tourist board in person, you will find they usually have an assortment of brochures covering everything you might need: hotels, restaurants, sightseeing information or anything general. If you are unable to visit, call them and request that they send you, by snail mail, general information brochures, maps, hotel and restaurant directories, and tour brochures. Do this far in advance, as the information could take 6–8 weeks to reach you. A great website to find tourist office website addresses and telephone numbers is *www.towd.com.*

You may also be able to get general information from a local travel agent. Find a TRAVEL AGENCY (see Chapter 12.1, *How to Find a Reliable Travel Agent*) that does vacation travel vs. one that specializes in corporate business. A vacation travel agency is more likely to have a supply of general information and TOUR BROCHURES. Ask for both escorted (host accompanies a bus load of people) and regular tour brochures for your destination. Part of your research has already been done in these brochures. A brochure for an "escorted" tour is usually put together by someone local and includes the most popular sightseeing places a tourist would want to visit. It also lists recommended hotels by category. These hotels have been checked out by the tour operator and have to be good enough to keep the wholesaler out of lawsuits. These hotels tend to be touristy group hotels and are a starting point for your hotel search. See the section on hotels for more details.

While you are at the travel agency, you can also spend a few minutes chatting with an agent to gain information. If the person is knowledgeable and takes time with you, then get their business card and book with them after you have done your research. Travel agents do not make any money giving you information. They may charge you a service fee to give you information and brochures. Quite often, this fee is applied toward the purchase of a trip if you return to book with them.

Using a Travel Guide as a Research Tool

The first TRAVEL GUIDE I look for is one that covers the general area, *GO EUROPE*, for example. Or, if the destination is popular, as is Orlando, there may be specific books about this area. A good example is *Birnbaum's 2003 Walt Disney World.*

I look at the table of contents to become familiar with the layout of the book. Then I head to the general information section and look for the "How to get there" or transportation section. It should list the airlines that fly there and which airport is best if there are multiple airports. I grab my writing material, either a notebook, pad, or index cards, and jot down the airlines that fly there and the name of the closest airport. I note "TRANSPORTATION" at the top. Next to the name of the airline, I write down the telephone number and the website address. Most guides list these somewhere, possibly in the back of the book. Otherwise, go to your Yellow Pages and look under "airlines" for their telephone numbers. Any Internet search engine can help you find the airline's web address. Try the airline name dot com. Most of them are listed this way.

While I'm in the transportation section, I look for any local transportation that I may need, such as a subway, train, bus or taxi. I note on an index card any special information, such as where to buy weekly train tickets, or what the tipping policy is in that country. You may have to look under a specific city for that information.

Then I go to the hotel section in the city I plan to visit. Each book is laid out differently. First I look for the general area I want to be in. Hopefully, the book lists the hotels by location and rating or category, i.e., tourist class, first class, etc. I then list the hotels on a sheet of paper, making a note of the ones that look interesting. These I will research first. Sometimes I use one index card per hotel and jot down key points that make it different from the other, for example, is there a pool on the roof. You can note the general rate range on the card.

At some point in my research, I make a detailed list of activities, places to visit, sightseeing, and restaurants. These go on index cards, usually by area. Then I only have to carry the index cards for the area I am visiting instead of the heavy guidebook. The index cards conveniently fit in my "fanny pak."

Before I am finished with the travel guide, I take a better look at any maps that may show street details. If they have hotels listed, that's a plus. Then it is easier to do my research by area. I check with the tourist board to see if they have a similar map or make a copy of the one in the book.

I go through several guides this way and eventually have the information I need for my trip on index cards. I pull out the hotel cards for further research on rates and availability.

Research: How to Get There

Once you have decided where to go, you then need to figure out how you'll get there. Will you fly or drive? Have you decided to take a cruise or travel across country by train? All of these modes of transportation are affected by other factors. Timing is one—when are you going, how much time do you have? Do you want to get there quickly by flying or will a leisurely train ride be part of the experience? Do you have lots of time and don't mind spending two days or more traveling to and from your destination?

Which Airlines Fly Nonstop to Your Destination? You could call each airline and ask if they fly to your destination. Most of the larger airlines probably do, via one of their hub cities. You could search each airline's website for the answer, but why waste the time? The easiest way to find which airlines fly nonstop to your destination is to call a travel agent and ask them to check their computer system. (A possible service fee may be charged.) Or you could go to the website: *www.sidestep.com* and do a quick search.

- What are the departure and arrival times of the flights?
- How many nonstop flights, if any, do they have?
- How long does the flight take?
- What is the lowest airfare offered at this time?
- Are there seats available on these flights?

Your next step is to check the availability and airfares of the flights. This is where the challenge comes in. Do you do it yourself or get some help from a travel agent?

Doing It Yourself

If you have lots of time on your hands, many packets of index cards and this book, you can do it yourself. Throughout this book are tips to help you "do it yourself." There are sections for surfing the web for airfares, hotels, and cars, as well as how to find a travel agent.

One last question: How do you know if you are getting the lowest airfare and best value for your dollar? Or is that two questions?

Answer: You probably don't. But a travel agent who is experienced in your destination will.

Part Three: All About Airlines

Chapter 8	Understanding the Airline Industry	59
Chapter 8.1	Airline Hub and Spoke System	69
Chapter 8.2	Anatomy of an Airfare	74
Chapter 8.3	Surf the Web for Airfares	84
Chapter 8.4	Sources for Airline Discounts	96
Chapter 8.5	How to Make an Airline Reservation	107

CHAPTER 8

Understanding the Airline Industry

The Airline Route System

Before you go online or call an airline, you should have some understanding of the airline route system. This will help save you time and money.

For example, if you once lived in Detroit, you probably have flown and collected frequent flyer miles on Northwest Airlines. But now you live in New York City and want to take a trip to Orlando. Your first call will probably be to Northwest Airlines because you are familiar with their service and have many unused frequent flyer miles. The reservation agent at Northwest says, yes, we fly there. You could fly out of LaGuardia to Detroit, change planes, and take another flight to Orlando. The airfare could be around $400. But if you had some knowledge of the airline route structure, you probably would not have called them first. The predominant airline that flies nonstop from New York City to Florida is Delta. If you called them, you would have found several nonstop flights a day and airfares as low as $165 roundtrip, if available.

The airlines in the United States and around the world are categorized according to their size.

Trunk Airlines/Major Airlines: The large domestic airlines, American, Continental, Delta, Northwest, United, and US Airways, are known as trunk carriers. This term is seldom used, but I am using it here to differentiate them from the smaller regional airlines. The trunk carriers' routes extend over the entire United States and beyond. Internationally they tend to be the "flag carrier" or country airline, such as British Airways or Air France.

Regional or Local Airlines: At one time these airlines were the small independent carriers serving less populated areas out of small regional airports. The cost to run flights out of these small airports tended to be unprofitable. As a result, it became essential for the survival of the regional airlines to create an alliance with the trunk carriers. These new alliances, such as American Eagle or Delta Express, have benefited everyone. The trunk airlines could offer flights to cities that were previously unprofitable to serve directly. At the same time, the regional carriers had passengers fed to them, mostly business passengers. The passenger now had access to better fares and cities that would most likely not have service because of the cost. Another benefit: the regional carriers had to adopt the safety standards of the trunk airline.

Unfortunately, since 9/11/01, and the instability of the airline industry, many of these small airports have fewer flights.

Small Airlines: There are a few airlines that fall in a category other than the trunk/major airlines, regional or "no frills" airlines. These few are unique in their own way.

One is America West Airlines, who primarily services Las Vegas and Phoenix. They are a full-service airline that can offer lower airfares because of the high demand for seats to Las Vegas.

Another is Midwest Express, a single-class premium-service airline. Their award-winning service includes, leather seats, gourmet food and freshly baked chocolate chip cookies. They primarily service flights through their hub city, Milwaukee, to most major U.S. cities.

"No Frills" or Discount Airlines

The last category of airline is "no frills"/discount airlines. This is a general term used to describe the services—or lack thereof—provided for the cheaper airfare. Once deregulation hit the travel industry, "no frills" or limited services, became the norm for new airlines.

Characteristics of "no frills" airlines:

- Electronic or paperless tickets
- All tickets are nonrefundable
- Generally sell one-way fares at a discount
- No advance seat assignments—get them at check-in
- No food service
- Beverages can be purchased on board
- Check-in time may be longer than usual
- Baggage may be limited, whether checked or carried on
- No frequent flyer miles
- Change penalty is cheaper. The big guys charge $100 to change a nonrefundable ticket. The "no frills" carriers generally charge $25
- Usually only confirmable via the web or phone
- Not in the travel agency computers.

A "no frills" airline strategy may be to offer fewer services in exchange for low airfares. This is a trade-off many people are willing to make to save a considerable amount of money on their airline tickets. Obviously this ploy works because these discount airlines seem to be flourishing, and new ones start up every month.

Normally a "no frills"/discount airline does heavy advertising in the cities they serve. Watch for billboards, newspaper, or radio advertising. Or you can call a local travel agency and ask them.

The survival of these "upstart," "no frills" airlines depends on their ability to survive the attack from the long-established trunk/major carriers. The major airlines initially lost a considerable amount of business to these "no frills" airlines. As a result, the major airlines go into direct competition with the "no frills" airlines on routes the majors had never intended to fly. They match the lower airfares of the "no frills" airlines and continue to "pay" frequent flyer miles. This behavior is to subtly force the "no frills" airlines out of business so the majors can charge more for an airline seat.

Case in point. From my observation as a travel agent, American Airlines has struggled to maintain their foothold in the JFK to San Francisco market. Their biggest competitor has been United Airlines, another major airline, who offers more nonstop flights per day. Then, along comes a new "no frills" airline called jetBlue. JetBlue flies JFK to Oakland, CA, another airport close to San Francisco and offers extremely cheap airfares with fewer restrictions. In the JFK to San Francisco market, American and United both loose hundreds of passengers to this cheaply priced airline. American must have felt so threatened by jetBlue that they have added flights on routes they have never flown nonstop. To directly compete with jetblue, American Airlines has added flights on the JFK to Oakland, CA route as well as JFK to Long Beach. But, due to low demand, American has discontinued JFK to Oakland flights as of March 01, 2003.

To press my point, let's talk airfares:

American Airlines JFK—Los Angeles	**jetBlue** JFK—Long Beach
Monday to Friday travel	Monday to Friday travel
$2200 roundtrip	$315 to $615 roundtrip
Fully refundable	NONrefundable
No change fees	$25 change fee
No advance purchase	No advance purchase
No minimum stay	No minimum stay
Offered on most economy seats	Price is subject to availability level

A roundtrip JFK to Los Angeles, Monday to Friday travel, costs over $2200, refundable. Nonrefundable fares are not offered unless you stay over a Saturday night. Enter jetBlue into the picture. Few businessmen can plan 7 days in advance and lock it in stone. But if you fly into the nearby Long Beach airport on jetBlue you can get a roundtrip airfare of $615, subject to availability and confirmable anytime in advance. AND THIS IS THE HIGHEST AIRFARE THEY SELL!! If the inventory was available for the cheapest airfare, you'd pay $332 roundtrip. Now American has added flights from JFK to Long Beach and has matched the $332 airfare. That's quite a difference from the original $2200 American charged prior jetBlue's arrival. Now do you understand why "no frills" airlines are such a threat to the major "expensive" airlines? For someone traveling once a year, and not collecting frequent flyer miles, this is a dramatic difference. I can pack a lunch and bring a book to save close to $2000!

Another point: if jetBlue succumbs (but I doubt they will) to the pressure of American's direct competition, you can guarantee that American would discontinue the cheaper airfares and return to the higher pre-jetBlue airfares. Several of the major airlines have used this strategy in the past. I'm sure they would repeat this practice.

AUTHOR'S NOTE

If you want to continue to have low airfares, fly the "no frills" airlines whenever you can. It keeps the major airlines' prices in check and stimulates competition.

One last note: in the past the "no frills" airlines were considered to be "fly-by-nights." Every month there would be a new start up and an old one would go bankrupt. Although it is difficult to stay in business in this post-9/11 era, the "no frills" airlines are not just surviving, they are thriving. It looks as if they will take over the small airlines category in the U.S. and around the world.

"No Frills" General Information

What follows is a brief description of the "no frills" airlines in the U.S.

American Trans Airways (TZ): HUB: Midway Airport Chicago. They are doing so well they have ordered 50 more planes and have a brand-new air terminal building at Midway Airport. They fly all over the U.S. Both American and Continental now also fly into Midway Airport to compete.

Reservations: 1-800-I-FLY-ATA

Website: *www.ata.com*

Airtran Airways (FL): HUB: Atlanta. Their biggest competition is Delta. They fly primarily east of the Mississippi River. They have received the FAA Diamond Award for maintenance and fly the new high tech Boeing 717 airplane. I recently flew this airline and was pleasantly surprised at their friendly, but limited, service. You can only get seat assignments at check-in, so get there early if you want a decent seat. I flew the new Boeing 717 and felt like I was in a new car. The décor was fresh, bright and roomy. The tray table, when open, did not pinch my lap. One factor that stuck out, everyone was treated the same. There was no passenger distinction based on amount paid, or frequent flyer status. I liked that. Air Tran also offers a oneway upgrade for $25. Check with reservations for details and when they are applicable.

Reservations: 1-800-AIR-TRAN,

In Atlanta 770-994-8258

Website: *www.airtran.com*

Delta's Song: Delta's new low-fare service. Song will replace Delta Express which was unable to survive because of high-priced salaries. Delta has started a new low-fare subsidiary to serve the Northeast to Florida markets. Song will be high tech with low fares. Watch for its launch in Spring 2003.

Website: *www.flysong.com* or *www.delta.com*

Frontier Airlines (F9): HUB: Denver. They operate short haul flights under 1½ hours. Frontier's strategy is to offer affordable airfares with full service including advance seat assignments, electronic ticketing, and "quality"' meals. They offer a corporate discount program. One note of distinction: their maintenance crew received the FAA Diamond Award for 3 times, 1999, 2001, 2002, for surpassing maintenance training requirements. They have ordered several new airplanes for delivery 2001–2003.

Reservations: 1-800-243-6297

Website: *www.frontierairlines.com*

jetBlue (B6): HUB: JFK/Kennedy Airport in New York City. They have quickly proven that an airline can offer cheap prices and be profitable. They offer low fares to cities in upstate NY and around the U.S. Amenities include brand-new Airbuses, blue leather seats, blue Terra chips for snacks, advance seat assignments and DirecTV at each seat. They provide connecting service to international flights. You must buy your ticket when you make your reservation and then it is nonrefundable. (No courtesy 24-hour hold) This airline is doing so well it just ordered another 100 Boeing 737 airplanes.

Reservations: 1-800-JET-BLUE
Website: *www.jetblue.com*

Southwest Airlines (WN): One of the U.S.'s major short haul low fare airlines and operates profitably. This is the airline with a sense of humor—just listen to the ads while on hold! Over 4 billion dollars in revenue, they serve 58 cities around the U.S. 25% of their revenue comes from their website bookings. They have won numerous awards for on-time service and fewest customer complaints. Fortune Magazine has listed them as one of the best 100 companies to work for. They must be doing something right!

This is the originator of the true "no frills" airline. At one time their airline tickets were cash register receipts. Now they have graduated to ticketless travel. They do not do advance seat assignments or take pets, and are famous for their hearty meals of peanuts. They do email your reservation though.

Reservations: 1-800-IFLY-SWA
Website: *www.southwest.com*

Sun Country Airlines (SY): HUB: Minneapolis/St. Paul (MSP). For a while after 9/11 they returned to charter service. Now they are back with scheduled service. Check their website for dates and cities.

They have both a First Class and an economy cabin and offer a corporate program called "Onefare." They fly from key U.S. cities to warm destinations for low fares. You must pay when you make your reservation. Confirmations are sent by fax.

Reservations: 1-800-FLY-N-SUN
Website: *www.suncountry.com*

Spirit Airlines (NK): Once a charter airline to casino cities, Spirit has grown into a regular scheduled airline offering low fares for limited services. They do not have a HUB city but have established key routes to popular resort or casino destinations.

Reservations: 1-800-772-7117
Website: *www.spiritair.com*

Vanguard: HUB: Kansas City. They are in Chapter 11 and looking for start-up money. It is rumored Hooters Restaurants may take it over. As if flight attendants didn't already sport an iffy persona.

International "No Frills" Airlines

It is difficult to keep track of the "no frills"' airlines around the world. As is the case in the U.S., new "no frills" airlines are cropping up all over the world. Check with one of the more popular travel search engines for new ones.

Within Europe

BMIBABY: a new low-cost airline from BMI British Midland. They fly from East Midland Airport, UK, to several Mediterranean cities. Check-in 2 hours prior to departure, with your booking reference number, identification, and lunch. You can buy snacks and drinks aboard. Interestingly enough, they will have a surcharge if you pay by credit card (this is illegal in the U.S.) no surcharge if you pay by debit card.

Reservations (UK) 0870-264-2229
Website: *www.bmibaby.com*

Buzz Air: a low-cost airline from the Dutch airline, KLM. They offer flights from London/Stansted airport to all over Europe. Book online, or via reservations in Europe. Terrific website, easy to use. Flight displays include 1–3 days of flight availability with prices. Purchase food on board. They also have car and hotel discounts, as well as destination information.

Website: *www.buzzaway.com*

Easyjet: another United Kingdom budget airline flying to various European cities. They merged with Go Airlines and now have the largest and most profitable "no frills" airline in Europe.

Website: *www.easyJet.com*

Flybe: British European: changing its business model to be a low-fare carrier with frills. Flights from London and Liverpool to Europe. They are partners in Continental's Onepass frequent flyer program.

Website: *www.flybe.com*

Ryanair: Europe's premier discount airline. You can only buy tickets online. Operates out of Dublin, several London airports, and Brussels, to many small airports around key European cities. They sell very cheap "use it or lose it fares" and higher fares that allow changes. You can buy coffee, drinks or snacks aboard. There is a small handling fee if you pay by credit card. No preassigned seating, only electronic tickets. They also have a hotel discount program through needahotel.com. Book either online or by phone.

In Ireland call 01-609-7881, UK call 0870-333-1231, other European cities, check website.

Website: *www.ryanair.com*

Virgin Express: Hub is Brussels. This "no frills" low-fare airline is part of Richard Branson's Virgin Group. Offers inexpensive flights to Madrid, Malaga, Faro, London/Heathrow, Milan, Rome and Copenhagen. No tickets, only a reservation number. Free coffee or tea, no meals except sandwiches on Spain and Italy flights. You can buy soda or drinks on board.

Website: *www.virgin-express.com*

Australia and New Zealand

Australian Airlines: A new "no frills" airline from Qantas to serve Asian destinations. Will start with flights from Cairns to several cities in Asia. Check website for new routes.

Reservations: within Australia: 1300 799 798

Website: *www.australianairlines.com.au*

Freedom Air: New Zealand to Tasmania "no frills" airline.

Website: *www.freedomair.com*

Air New Zealand–Express Class: Air New Zealand has changed their domestic route system into a "no frills" airline. They've eliminated business class and reduced airfares from 20 to 60%. They offer a 30 second check-in kiosk for people without baggage. Go to the Air New Zealand website and look for "Express Class."

Website: *www.airnz.co.nz*

Virgin Blue: operated by Sir Richard Branson's UK based company. Offers discounts within Australia.

Website: *www.virginblue.com*

Canada

Tango Air: a "no frills" airline launched by Air Canada. They fly from Canadian cities to Florida.

Website: *www.flytango.com*

CHAPTER 8.1

Airline Hub and Spoke System

The second best marketing plan the airlines have come up with is the HUB AND SPOKE SYSTEM. (The frequent flyer program is the first.) Both the trunk and regional airlines have developed their route system based on a bicycle wheel-type layout called the hub and spoke system. They schedule flights to go via these special hub cities to maximize seats sold, increase revenues, keep passengers on their airline, and build brand loyalty. The schedules are developed so that you can go from any one city in the system to another on the same airline. Very rarely will you have to change planes and switch airlines to get to your destination. There is very little scheduling using multiple airlines, primarily because it is not cost effective (you would need to buy two tickets instead of one). To get the best fare you need to stay on the same airline.

What Is a Hub City?

A hub city is usually in a large populated area or a city where the airline thinks there is an enormous potential for growth. The airline schedules flights to many cities in and out of this hub airport. Usually, the major airlines with larger planes operate the longer flights. The regional carriers operate the shorter flights with smaller planes.

A hub city usually has a large concentration of flights for that one airline, often with little competition from other airlines. When this lack of competition exists, the airfares to this city are usually over-priced. If one of the major airlines starts to fly to another major airline's hub city, the airfares may come down, but usually not for long. The business traveler may want his favorite airline to fly to that hub city, but he will have to pay for the privilege. If a "no frills" discount airline starts flying to a hub monopoly city, the fares may go down in the beginning. Eventually the major airline may not see the "no frills" carrier as a threat and will raise prices to what the market (i.e., business traveler) can bear.

Tips for Cheaper Airfares

- When planning an itinerary, it is essential to know what the hub cities are for each of the large airlines. This will save you research time and money. Often fares through connecting cities/hubs can be cheaper than the nonstop. For example, if you were flying New York City/JFK to Phoenix, you might find a roundtrip nonrefundable fare of $406.50 on the nonstop on America West Airlines. But if you fly on a connection via Dallas on American Airlines the fare could be around $240.
- You should also be familiar with the routings of the "no frills" airlines for a comparison. See the previous chapter for information about "no frills"/discount airlines.

Benefits of a Hub and Spoke System

- It is easier to transfer passengers and their bags from one flight to another in a timely fashion.
- The airline that issued the ticket keeps the entire revenue from the ticket. They do not have to share revenue with another airline. Keeps the cost down for the traveler.
- The airline knows when its passengers are delayed and can hold another plane at the gate to await the connecting passengers.
- Improves reliability of connecting flights.
- Ability to reroute passengers if delayed, especially during bad weather. They can reroute you via a different hub city.

Disadvantages of a Hub

- Monopoly: keeps the airfare price in the control of the hub airline, usually a higher price than in competitive markets.

Hub Cities for "No Frills" Airlines

AMERICAN TRANSAIR /ATA: Chicago: Midway Airport

AIRTRAN AIRWAYS: Atlanta

FRONTIER: Denver

JETBLUE: New York City: Kennedy

SOUTHWEST AIRLINES: Dallas: Love Field, Phoenix, Las Vegas, Baltimore and others

SUN COUNTRY AIRLINES: Minneapolis/St Paul, MSP

SPIRIT AIRLINES: No one hub, key resort cities, direct flights

Hub Cities for Larger Airlines

AMERICAN AIRLINES: New York: Kennedy, LaGuardia; Chicago/O'Hare, Dallas/Ft. Worth, Miami, Los Angeles, St. Louis (TWA), San Francisco, San Jose, CA, San Juan, Puerto Rico

AMERICA WEST: Las Vegas

CONTINENTAL: Newark, Cleveland, Houston

DELTA: Atlanta, Cincinnati, Orlando, Salt Lake City

MIDWEST EXPRESS: Milwaukee

NORTHWEST: Detroit, Minneapolis/St. Paul, Memphis

US AIRWAYS: Pittsburgh, Philadelphia, Charlotte

UNITED: Chicago/O'Hare, Denver, Washington/Dulles, San Francisco

IF AIRLINES SOLD PAINT

BUYING PAINT FROM A HARDWARE STORE:

Customer: Hi, how much is your paint?
Clerk: We have regular quality for $12 a gallon and premium for $18. How many gallons would you like?
Customer: Five gallons of regular quality, please.
Clerk: Great. That will be $60 plus tax.

BUYING PAINT FROM AN AIRLINE:

Customer: Hi, how much is your paint?
Clerk: Well, sir, that all depends.
Customer Depends on what?
Clerk: Well, there are a lot of things.
Customer: How about just giving me an average price?
Clerk: Wow, that's just too hard a question. The lowest price is $9 a gallon, and we have 150 prices up to about $200 a gallon.
Customer: What's the difference in the paint?
Clerk: Oh, there isn't any difference; it's all the same paint.
Customer: Well then, I'd like some of that $9 paint.
Clerk: Well, first I need to ask you a few questions. When do you intend to use it?
Customer: I want to paint tomorrow which is my day off.
Clerk: Sir, the paint for tomorrow is the $200 paint.
Customer: What!! When would I have to paint in order to get the $9 paint?
Clerk: That would be in three weeks, but you will also have to agree to start painting before Friday and continue painting until at least Sunday.
Customer: You've got to be kidding!
Clerk: Sir, we don't kid around here. Of course, I would have to check to see if we have any of that paint available before I could sell it to you.
Customer: You have shelves full of the stuff; I can see it right there. What do you mean check to see if you can sell it to me?

Clerk:	**Just because you can see it doesn't mean that we have it. It may be the same paint, but we only sell a certain number of gallons on any given weekend. Oh, and by the way, the price just went to $12.**
Customer:	**What!! You mean the price just went up while we were talking?!**
Clerk:	**Yes sir. You see, we change prices and rules thousands of times a day, and since you haven't actually walked out the store with your paint yet, we just decided to change. Unless you want the same thing to happen again, I would suggest that you get on with your purchase. How many gallons do you want?**
Customer:	**I don't know exactly. I guess I will buy a little extra**
Clerk:	**Oh no, sir, you can't do that. If you buy the paint and then don't use it, you will be liable for penalties and possible confiscation of the paint you already have.**
Customer:	**What!**
Clerk:	**That's right. We can sell you enough paint to do your kitchen, bathroom, hall, and north bedroom, but if you stop painting before you do the bedroom, you will be in violation of our tariffs.**
Customer:	**But what does it matter to you whether I use all the paint? I already paid you for it!**
Clerk:	**There is no point in getting upset; that's just the way it is. We make plans based upon the idea that you will use all the paint, as you have agreed to do, and when you don't, it just causes us all sorts of problems.**
Customer:	**This is crazy! I suppose something terrible will happen if I don't keep painting until after Saturday night!**
Clerk:	**Yes, sir, it will.**
Customer:	**Well, that does it! I'm going to another company to buy my paint.**
Clerk:	**That won't do you any good, sir. We all have the same rules. Oh, and thanks for flying, er I mean painting with our airline.**

CHAPTER 8.2
Anatomy of an Airfare

EVERY FLIGHT HAS A VARIETY OF PRICES OFFERED FOR THE SAME SEAT.

The price you pay depends on several factors, which include:

- How far in advance you purchase your ticket
- Whether it is a one-way or a nonrefundable roundtrip ticket
- Whether you stay over a Saturday night
- Where you purchase your ticket

Another key factor is how many seats remain in availability on that flight at the time when you make your reservation. What is the current tariff projection for this flight/date? (How much money would the flight make?) Is the date of travel prior to a holiday? What is the history of no-shows for the past 30 days, or the same day last year? How many seats are allowed for overbooking? (Are your confused yet? I know I am!) This is a highly developed system the airlines have created called "YIELD MANAGEMENT." Each airline uses different guidelines for the revenue expectation of a flight. American Airlines might offer a nonrefundable fare for 80% of the seats on a flight, while a competing airline such as United Airlines might discount only 60% of its seats for the same routing.

To give you an idea of what you are up against when searching for a discounted airline seat, I will show you what a computer reservation system's, availability screen looks like. Then I'll give you a list of SOME of the airfares on one specific flight. The information in an airline computer or travel agent GDS gives a clearer picture of what is available on a bunch of flights at a given time. If you are searching online, you get only one tiny piece of the puzzle at one time.

Travel Agent's GDS Computer Screen

115APR LGAMCO1P		entry typed in				
response:						
15APR MON LGA/EDT		MCO/EDT‡0				
1DL 257	F7 A7 Y7 B7 M7	LGAMCO	8	145P	416P
	H7 Q0 K0 L0 U0	M80	S	0	DCA /E
2DL 421	F7 A7 Y7 B7 M7	LGAMCO	9	1210P	241P
	H7 Q3 K0 L0 U0	763	L	0	DCA /E
3AA 2275	F7 Y7 B7 K7 H7	LGAMCO	N	1115A	159P
	M7 Q7 V7 S3 N2 L0	763	L	0	DCA /E

This availability: 1 15APR LGA MCO 1P, is for flight departures on April 15, LaGuardia/New York City to Orlando around 1:00 P.M. The "1" at the beginning is a code to tell the computer that what follows is a request for availability.

Only 3 of 6 lines that appear on the screen are shown in the example above. Each flight displayed has a variety of prices offered for sale for the same seat. An experienced travel agent can look at this screen and immediately see what's available. The letters with numbers 1 to 7 after them have seats available. Any letter with a "0" after it has no seat in that inventory. For example, let's look at the flight listed on line 3:

3AA 2275	F7 Y7 B7 K7 H7	LGAMCO	N	1115A	159P
	M7 Q7 V7 S3 N2 L0	763	L	0	DCA /E

- **3:** line 3 out of 6 (only 3 shown above).
- **AA 2275:** American Airlines flight number 2275
- **F7:** F is first class; there are at least 7 seats available in this inventory. This GDS lists a maximum of 7 seats. (SABRE)
- **LGAMCO:** routing, New York City/LaGuardia to Orlando.
- **N:** This is the percent this flight was on time for the last 30 days. N: Denotes that there was no statistic recorded for the last 30 days of departures. Generally a number of 1 to 9 is listed. This represents a 10 to 90 percent on-time factor. The two Delta flights on lines 1 and 2 have an on-time percentage of 8 and 9 (80% and 90%), respectively. If a flight has a lousy on-time percentage, the airline might change the flight number to bypass this statistic. Hence the N. Also a new flight will have an **N**.

- **1115A 159P:** departure and arrival times
- **763 L 0 DCA:** type of plane "763"—a Boeing 767; a lunch meal offered to both first and economy cabins; number of stops, in this case nonstop; DCA: "Direct Connect Availability"—the travel agent can look directly into the airlines' computer system for last seat availability, bypassing the GDS availability.
- **/E:** offers electronic ticketing.

At the time of this writing, the following is the breakdown of the one-way fares offered for sale on this ONE flight AA 2275, LaGuardia to Orlando. These economy class inventories (or buckets): Y7, B7, K7, H7, M7, Q7, V7, S3, N2, L0, indicate the variety of prices for the same seat. There are also many roundtrip fares offered but I won't go into them here.

Nonrefundable One-Way Airfares

L—$ 84.50 "L0"	sold out, "L0" above
N—129.50 "N2"	2 seats available
V—135.50 "V7"	at least 7 seats available
Q—167.50 "Q7"	at least 7 seats available
M—201.50 "M7"	at least 7 seats available
H—365.50 "H7"	at least 7 seats available
K—247.50 "K7"	at least 7 seats available

Refundable One-Way Airfares

B—481.50 "B7"	at least 7 seats available
Y—612.50 "Y7"	at least 7 seats available

A display such as this makes it relatively easy for the experienced GDS user to quickly find discounted seats. I look for the letter to the right with seats available. This is usually the lowest price available. We only get one routing/direction (i.e., New York City to Orlando in this example) at a time but it is still easier than getting a listing of roundtrip flights that don't match your time guidelines or airports.

Please note, the prices listed above were for prices in place at time of writing and may not be in effect when you read this.

What Is a Nonrefundable Airfare?

Every flight has a variety of fares offered for the same seat. But in general, if your airline ticket is under $750, it is probably nonrefundable. The exceptions are in short-haul markets where the refundable economy fares are approximately $300 to $500 one-way.

If you are looking for a discounted fare, more than likely you will be purchasing a nonrefundable/"use it or lose it" airfare. It is the trade off you will have to make to get the discount: lots of rules and restrictions. This is why it is imperative you have your guidelines set before you go searching for a discount. One key rule: most discounted airfares require you to purchase your ticket within 24 hours or possibly immediately. If you purchase online, you can't make a reservation without purchasing the ticket at that moment. You are not even offered the 24 hours that you get elsewhere. (You might have 24 hours if you call the airline by telephone or book the same itinerary through a travel agent.)

General Rules of Nonrefundable Airfares

Every airfare has a "tariff filing" reference number attached to it. These rules are the general guidelines established by the airline's pricing/tariff department. There are many variations to every rule, especially the nonrefundable airfares. I will give you the general rules that usually pertain to most nonrefundable airfares for the major and small airlines.

Nonrefundable: Now "Use It or Lose Fares"

The latest change to nonrefundable tickets is that you must use it as written. It is only valid for the flight and date written on the ticket. In the past, if you didn't use your ticket, you could use the value of it, less the $100 penalty fee towards another ticket within the U.S. within one year. Now, you MUST change the date to any date within the next 10 months (airline computers only load flights 330 days in advance). PRIOR TO the date written on your ticket. You will have to pay the $100 penalty fee and any additional airfare to make this change. If you don't make the change and pay the penalty fee prior to the departure date written on the ticket, you will lose the entire value of the ticket. And, if you chose the wrong future date, you will have to pay the $100 penalty fee again, plus any additional airfare. Every time you change your ticket you are subject to the $100 penalty fee and any additional airfare that may apply.

AUTHOR'S NOTE

The impact of the 9/11/01 terrorist assault has taken a devastating toll on the airline and travel industry. Many companies, especially airlines, are filling Chapter 11 bankruptcy. To avoid losing your money, book less than 60 days prior to departure and pay by credit card. Every airline has been hit financially and is struggling to survive. Protect yourself and pay by credit card.

Fare Purchase Date

24-Hour Purchase Rule: Most nonrefundable airfares require that the ticket be purchased within "24 hours." Actually, this means by midnight of the next day, or by the listed advance purchase date of the airfare, whichever comes first. For example, if the fare has a 14-day advance purchase requirement and your departure date is 14 days from today, your ticket must be purchased/issued today. You do not have the "24-hour" rule. You do have until midnight tonight to purchase it.

THIS 24-HOUR RULE is necessary for the airline to make sure you intend to use the reservation you have booked. Otherwise, your seat goes back into inventory for someone else to buy. If there is no ticket number message in the reservation, most airline computers automatically cancel the reservation by the ticket purchase date. Exceptions are made for the very frequent, "Frequent Flyers."

Because of the volatility of airfares and the flexibility of computers, you may want to purchase your ticket on the same day you make your reservation. If the price changes, and you are not using a travel agent, you will have to pay the higher fare.

I have found that airfares can change within seconds. I once was issuing a group of 30 people booked on one reservation (PNR). I used an automated entry that allowed me to make one command and all 30 tickets would be issued one after the other. The whole ticketing process took approximately 1 minute to issue 30 tickets. When the computer was finished, I looked at the ticketing accounting data and saw that half the tickets printed out $25 cheaper. The airline had updated the airfare and it hit my computer system while the system was in the ticketing process. The airfare had been lowered! This was great news for my client, but more work for me. I voided out the higher-priced tickets and issued them at the cheaper airfare. My client was able to take advantage of the fickleness of the airline pricing strategy.

In this Computer Age, all an airline has to do to change the airfare, i.e., cancel/remove it, increase it, decrease it, is to electronically send the fare message to APTCO (the airlines tariff system), who then transfers the updated fare message to all the GDSs and airline computer systems. Previously, it was done at night; but now it can happen anytime throughout the day, as in the example above. What was quoted to you at 2:15 P.M. could have changed by 2:30 P.M.

If your travel agent catches the change in pricing within the 24-hour rule, they can possibly get authorization to ticket at the lower fare even if the fare was cancelled. If you purchase your ticket elsewhere, it is unlikely you would be able to take advantage of the lower fare.

Advance Purchase Requirements

Most nonrefundable airfares require you to purchase your ticket by a specific date to be valid. It could be 3, 7, 10, 14, 21, 30 days in advance. The most common ones are 7 and 14 days. There is no general rule for the lowest fare. Plan a month ahead to get the lowest rate. For holiday or school vacations, travel planning a minimum of 6-9 months in advance is recommended.

Most markets have many advance purchase fares for sale. In the same market, you could have a 7-, 14-, or 21-day fare: all are different prices and are booked in different inventories/buckets. Usually any of these fares can be combined with any of the others. If the lowest fare, a 21-day advance purchase fare, is available on the outbound flight and is sold out on the return flight, you could combine it with another nonrefundable category, possibly a 14-day, that is available. *This is why you get so many different quotes from different sources for the same flight.* The source you use to book your ticket, whether online, by telephone, or through a travel agent, may use a different computer link that gives different available inventories. The truest inventory is the response from your chosen airline's own computer system. Most travel agency's computer systems have this direct access ability, but not every travel agent using it knows how or where to look to get the most accurate response.

Capacity Controlled Inventory

All nonrefundable fares have a specific number of seats per flight that are allotted to that fare. Once all the seats in that fare inventory, or "bucket," are sold out, the next higher airfare "bucket" will apply. Most flights have many different airfare "buckets" available for sale. This depends on the cities in the routing and other airline competition. (See the example of the travel agent GDS computer screen at the beginning of this chapter.)

Minimum/Maximum Stay

Most nonrefundable airfares have a minimum stay of one Saturday night. Las Vegas has a 2-day minimum stay. Most roundtrip airfares have a maximum stay of 30 days. Certain higher nonrefundable airfares may have a longer maximum stay. Every market is different. Ask or verify the fare rules before you purchase your ticket.

Change Fees—"Use It or Lose It" Fares

Effective January 01, 2003, the airlines have changed the rules about changing tickets. The new rule requires that you make any changes PRIOR TO the date written on your ticket. If you wait to change your ticket to a date later, the ticket has no value—you've lost your money.

If you want to change the departure date, keep in mind you must also satisfy the advance purchase requirement. (See above.) If you cannot leave on that date, and want to retain a portion of the value of your ticket, pick a date within the next 10 months, a date you might want to travel. You will have to pay a $100 penalty fee to do this. Otherwise, you lose the entire value of the ticket.

All nonrefundable airfares have an airline-imposed penalty fee. Other than the "no frills" airlines, the penalty fee for domestic flights is $100 to change the return flight. The "no frills" airlines charge $25 to $50. Verify with your airline. International airfares generally charge $150 to $200 to change the *return* flight.

If you change the *departure* date, your ticket is no longer valid and you have to purchase a new one. You make a new reservation and price your itinerary based on the new information. Then you take the price of the original ticket, subtract the $100 penalty fee and apply any balance to the new ticket price. If your old airfare is lower that the new airfare, you will pay an additional amount to cover this difference.

See the chapter, *What to Do If You Can't Go,* for details.

Summary of Nonrefundable Rules

- Nonrefundable, means that you cannot get your money back.
- Purchase within 24 hours of booking or by the advance purchase date of fare.
- Advance purchase required, 7, 14 days, etc.
- Capacity controlled inventory.
- Minimum or Saturday night stay required on major airlines.
- Generally, maximum stay 30 days.
- There is a penalty fee to change the ticket.
- Changes must be done prior to date printed on ticket or you forfeit your money.

Understanding the Electronic Ticket Process

As we get further into the Computer Age, the airline industry devised a process to make ticketing easier for them, not the general public. It is more cost effective for the airlines to issue "paperless" or electronic tickets for the obvious reason—to handle less paper. The use of electronic tickets has also reduced the waiting time for processing tickets at airline ticket counters. In the beginning, when electronic tickets were new, it could be difficult to transfer your ticket to another airline when rerouting was necessary. As technology evolves, the airlines have developed an electronic ticket database that is accessible to multiple airlines. This makes it easier for the airline to reroute you if your flight is cancelled. As a result, paper tickets will eventually be eliminated.

What Is an Electronic Ticket or Ticketless Travel?

Electronic ticket, ETR, e-ticket, paperless or ticketless travel are interchangeable terms. An electronic ticket is a computer message in your airline reservation that shows you have PAID for a seat on specific flights. The only proof you may receive from an airline is a copy of the itinerary with the reservation number via email or fax. If you purchased your ticket from a travel agency, you should receive, by snail mail, a printed copy of the itinerary and a passenger receipt as proof of purchase. This passenger receipt is an actual copy of the electronic message in your reservation. If you purchased your ticket online or from the airline directly, you may not receive a copy in advance. When you check in for your flight, you will receive a paper boarding pass. It may or may not be a copy of the electronic ticket. If it does not have the fare on it, ask for a passenger copy of your electronic ticket. Other than the "no frills" airlines, this boarding pass usually is a printed picture of your paid airline ticket. DO NOT THROW IT AWAY—SAVE IT. It is proof that you traveled on that flight.

The "no frills" airlines do not print copies of electronic tickets. Your email or faxed itinerary is your only proof of purchase. Their boarding passes do not have any information on it other than your seat number.

Several of the airlines are either no longer issuing paper tickets or charging a $20 to $25 fee to have one printed from an electronic ticket reservation. The airlines are attempting to wean the traveler away from paper tickets. The major airlines will be phasing out paper tickets altogether by the end of 2003.

Benefits of an Electronic Ticket

To the Airline

Handle Less Paper: everything: reservation, frequent flyer information, purchased ticket information, is in a computer message for anyone at the airline or travel agency to retrieve and look at at any time (contains a programmed "in use" message in case of multiple viewing).

Increased Cash Flow: unused tickets are paid for and remain in the computer system. Until these tickets are "printed out" and refunded or reused by the traveler, the airline has use of this money. Many tickets are forgotten by the traveler and remain in the computer indefinitely. *The traveler has unwittingly donated several hundreds of dollars to the airline.*

Ease of Check-in Process: You present your identification to the agent at check-in. The agent can then retrieve your reservation information and print out a boarding pass. There is less handling of negotiable documents in the form of paper tickets.

To the Traveler

- Reservations can be made by phone or online.
- Tickets can be purchased by phone or online.
- Delivery or mailing of tickets is no longer under any time pressure.
- You only need the confirmation number/record locator to check in for a flight, plus photo identification.
- No tickets to lose, leave at home, or misplace.
- You no longer have to go in person to the airline ticket counter to change and reissue your ticket (Unless reissuing a paper ticket purchased online).
- Airline ticket agent cannot remove the wrong flight coupon from your ticket.

Disadvantages of Electronic Tickets

For You

- If you purchase a NONREFUNDABLE ticket it will remain in the airline computer system indefinitely. Unless you use it as scheduled, or change it, the airline will retain its value. If you forget you purchased it or neglect to change it prior to the departure date written on it, you have donated it to the airline.
- If you have a FULLY REFUNDABLE ticket, the airline will credit the credit card used as payment after 30 days. If it was paid for by something other than a credit card, it will remain in the computer.
- If the flight you are on is cancelled or delayed, you have to get a "paper ticket" printed out before you can use it on another airline. This will be the case until all the airlines have access to the electronic ticket database.
- If the airline goes out of business, you have to call or go to that airline and request a "paper ticket" be printed out before they shut their doors. Without the physical ticket, you are unable to make any refund claim with your credit card company. See Chapter 14, *What to Do If You Can't Go.*

CHAPTER 8.3
Surf the Web for Airfares

I admit it.

I'm spoiled.

Using an airline computer reservation system (GDS) for almost 25 years has jaded my experience with surfing the Internet. I'm used to getting answers to my queries within seconds, not minutes. I'm used to getting an answer directly related to my request, not some obscure reply. I find surfing the web total torture, especially when I'm looking for a travel product. I bet you feel the same way too.

With all the comparing I've done for the lowest airfares, the travel agent GDS computer that I use (SABRE) has been the best source for the best fare. Now the airlines claim the cost of selling seats through the travel agent GDS computer is more expensive than through various websites. As an excuse, the airlines say they do not want to give travel agents the specially negotiated deeper discounted web-only fares. Well, maybe, in today's market, the cost per ticket is cheaper through an airline website, but are the airlines ready to add all the extra personnel needed to handle the questions and changes from web bookings (not likely), questions that were previously answered by travel agents? Are the airlines ready for the added advertising expense of reaching one person at a time instead of reaching an industry that has been their (now free) sales force, the travel agent industry? Case in point: How many *orbitz.com* pop-up ads have you seen online, advertisements on TV, or billboards, etc.? I bet that has cost a bundle.

Now the dogfights have started. There are several companies developing software to link the web-only fares with the GDSs. With time, we will see another metamorphosis of travel computer technology both on the travel agent side and the general public side. The synonym for travel is: "change."

AUTHOR'S NOTE

Any website, other than an airline, that sells airline tickets is a "travel agency." In order for a company to issue an airline ticket, they must be "licensed" to do so by ARC, Airlines Reporting Corp. The travel search engines like Orbitz, Expedia, Travelocity or others are *travel agencies* and negotiate booking deals with the individual airlines to get income, just like your local travel agent. You will also start to see various websites assessing "booking fees" to cover expenses just like your local travel agent does, by charging a "service fee" for the same thing. They are in the same boat as a travel agency, but the online travel websites and the airlines do not offer much in the way of customer service.

Where Should You Begin?

I have tried several of the travel sites and find them all to be tedious at best. No one particular travel website gives you all the information in one place. Search several websites to get a "feel" for what's out there. Take notes (try using index cards) on the best fares, airline and flights and which travel website gave you the choice. Keep in mind that not all of the travel search engines check for the actual availability of a flight. You might get a cheap airfare on a flight and only find out that it is sold out when you try to book it. Read that website's rules or call customer service and ask where they get their information. Know how that particular travel website searches.

Various websites are continuously updating the performance of their sites. I have seen a dramatic difference in several travel websites, especially *priceline.com*. If you haven't visited one lately, go back and try it again. It might now work better or offer additional products.

I would approach my surfing in this order. *There is a detailed explanation of each in the section that follows:*

1. ***www.sidestep.com***: By using this plug-in, it will launch a comparison search when you request information from one of the other major travel websites.
2. Once you have downloaded the Sidestep plug-in, go to ***www.expedia.com*** and run your search. Compare your results. There are others that work almost as well but have slight differences that remove them from my choice list. See the website listing that follows for reasons.
3. **Travel agent:** Their computer systems have access to last seat availability. They also can check other sources for web-only airfares and can suggest alternate routings that the computers don't have programmed. You'll get a level of customer service that the websites and airlines cannot provide.
4. **"No frills" airlines:** If they serve your area, check them out just in case they are not in *Sidestep.com*'s or *expedia.com*'s airline list.

By organizing your travel search in this order you will cover most of the options available in the least amount of time. You no longer need to spend 15 hours searching for the best airfare. My latest comparison search

AUTHOR'S NOTE

Prices change repeatedly day by day, hour by hour. Do your research in one sitting, then go back the next day and redo it if you have the "advance purchase" time. Compare your results. Many times I make a reservation for a client and go back to ticket it the next day and find that the price has dropped. Also the reverse happens—the price increases. If a travel agent catches the price increase within the 24-hour ticketing rule, they can usually get the cheaper fare authorized. If you have not purchased your ticket through a travel agent, you will not be eligible for this "fare protection." If you buy your ticket online you must purchase it at the time you make your reservation. You do not have time to think about it.

of 9 websites plus my GDS took about 1½ hours. (I was also going back and forth comparing results and making notes.)

A brief background on several of the travel search engines follows.

As with any travel search, use the information gathered as a starting point in your research. See what they come up with. I found fares I liked, but not the scheduling, even though alternate flights and fares closer to my guidelines were available on the dates chosen. I searched SABRE, my airline computer (GDS) first, for the best fares and flights. Then I checked the various travel booking engines to see what they offered me. The results were startling. They seldom gave my specific option as a choice!!

Sidestep.com's Plug-in Browser

Before you do any travel research on the web, load this useful tool. Go to: *www.sidestep.com* and download their free plug-in program, which safely attaches itself to your Internet browser.

This Silicon Valley tech company has developed a unique COMPARISON search engine program that searches most of the major websites for the best travel deals including web-only fares. *Sidestep.com* looks through other travel search engines, airlines, hotels or car companies for matches to your requests and gives you many choices based on your guidelines.

In order to use *Sidestep.com*, you need to load their program on your MS Internet Explorer browser. It currently works with Windows 95 and higher and Microsoft Internet Explorer 5.0 and higher. Other browsers and operating systems are being developed. You can update your MS Internet Explorer to the latest version by downloading the upgrade for free from: *www.microsoft.com/windows/ie.*

Go to their website *www.Sidestep.com* and click on one of the many links to their download. Once you have downloaded the Sidestep plug-in browser, you will be prompted to restart your computer. After you have done this, launch your Internet browser and type in the Internet address of the travel website you want to search (i.e., *www.expedia.com*).

Sidestep.com can run a parallel search when you input travel guidelines into one of the other travel websites such as *expedia.com* or *travelocity.com*. When you enter the dates, times and cities, Sidestep usually opens automatically. If you want a COMPARISON search, click on the "search with Sidestep" button. Sidestep will run a search based on the guidelines input into the other vendor. If it doesn't open automatically, click on the Sidestep icon on the toolbar. (It looks like a coin with a plane on it.) When Sidestep gives you your options, you can compare the results side-by-side with the other website.

Sidestep.com is relatively fast. You can get 30 or so choices in about a minute. Sidestep also negotiates its own "web-only" fares with several airlines.

It is also very easy to change your search guidelines. Just click on the drop-down box and you can change you present results by price, airline, stops, arrival time or departure time. You can change travel guidelines by clicking on the spyglass icon and requesting a new search. Results again, in about a minute.

Sidestep.com is designed to give you a wide range of options. Sometimes the airfares can vary by hundreds of dollars by using an alternate airport. For example, I was astonished to find an option through Sidestep that did not come up in my agency computer. I requested a search, NYC to Los Angeles, departing on Monday returning on Thursday, no Saturday night stay. My computer showed a price of $2263.50 on the major airlines nonstop flights. Sidestep found an alternate airport of Ontario with a nonstop JFK flight on jetBlue for $295. Wow! What a difference. You will not find this option in the GDSs or the travel search engines that use GDSs because they do not have Ontario programmed as an alternative airport to Los Angeles. A 50-mile drive might be worth the $2000 savings. Thanks to Sidestep, I had the option.

However, I have also noticed inconsistencies in Sidestep's search results. Sometimes it misses obvious lower fares by skipping an airline or two and defaulting to an online agency it has an arrangement with (like *orbitz.com*). Or possibly the airline website was "down"—unavailable at the moment the request was made. (I've seen this happen.) Wait a few minutes then re-search. It may bring up different results for the same guidelines. As with other searches, use as a guideline and check again, the next day or so.

For the latest information about surfing airline websites
send an e-mail to
tips@discounttravelwisdom.com

Other Travel Search Engines

To help you through the maze of online "travel search engines," I will give you my observations. If you are working with one of these and feel comfortable with them, continue to do so. If you are looking for a new "travel search engine," look through the list and see which one might work for you. As always, *this information is subject to change* as the websites are continuously updating. You might want to go back to an old site and see if it has changed. Or you might want to try a new one.

Cheaptickets.com

Still not a good site.
1-888-922-8849
Cheaptickets has improved its website but still has a long way to go to compete with the better websites. You now can search and see flight details without having to log-on. Roundtrip itineraries are offered instead of one direction at a time. My specific flight combinations seldom came up together. Cheaptickets seems to use certain airlines quite often and skips the big boys who are also available at similar or lower prices. But, be sure to load the *Sidestep.com* plug-in browser for a flight listing comparison. Cheaptickets does not have jetBlue in their pool of airlines.

Expedia.com

ONE OF THE BEST TRAVEL SEARCH ENGINES.
1-800-EXPEDIA for customer support
I give this website high marks!! They keep getting better and better! Repeatedly, this website gives the best options and best prices. It's easy to use and easy to revise. Load *Sidestep.com* and then go to *expedia.com* to start your search. Most of the time both sites will give you similar responses. Expedia does NOT require you to log-on to view flight information. They have a "build your own trip" module where they give you the departing flight schedules first. Pick one and move on to the return flight. Use the back button or forward button to maneuver between departing and returning flight schedules to get the itinerary you want. You can choose how you want the display to appear—by lowest price, departure time, arrival time or flying time. One note: the initial display gives flights

based on lowest price then early morning departure times. Look down the list and find the departure time you requested. Once you have the flights and price you want, you will then have to log-on. They sometimes offer ground transportation, sightseeing tours, and flight protection insurance, all of which must be selected from the page they are listed on. You cannot go "back" and add one in after you have left the page. You can also choose your seat assignments. There is a bidding site called "Flight Fare Matcher." See the section on bidding for an airline seat.

Farechase.com

No longer a travel search engine. It now designs software for other travel companies.

Hotwire.com

A "blind buy" so/so website.
Not a great choice. Must log-on to request a price. You give your dates of travel only, times not allowed. They respond with a price. You have one hour to buy, and then they give you the airline and times of departure. I got the same price, and lower, on Sidestep. Hotwire's tickets are nonrefundable, no changes allowed. Why buy from them when you can buy from the airline direct and have some customer service if needed? I don't see how this site will continue to exist when you can do better elsewhere and not have the heavy restrictions.

Lowestfare.com

Unfortunately they were unable to survive the selling of airline tickets without being paid a commission by the airlines. *priceline.com* has purchased the domain name and trademark and now uses it as another link to their "name your own price" product.

Onetravel.com

1-800-929-2523
Current website is not very good.
Supposedly a new one is in development. Original site was price-driven, not time specific and gave 4 choices. And misses the cheaper major airline

lower fares. New site, in beta test at present, is supposedly more user friendly. You now should be able to request a search that includes departure or arrival times, sort by price, airline, or shortest flight. If you haven't visited this site lately try again. Or better yet, try one of the good ones.

Orbitz.com

1-888-656-4546 for customer care
Orbitz.com has now added a 'log-in" which has dropped them from my recommended list. This is a privacy issue—if you log-on, they can track every move you make.

This website seems to offer the lowest fares on one of their 5 partners. If there is a web-only fare available, it will come up first and will be marked with "Orbitzsaver." Load *Sidestep.com* in case there is a lower fare on one of the other airlines.

Orbitz.com is financially supported and designed by the 5 largest "full service" U.S. airlines: American, Continental, Delta, Northwest, and United. In my opinion, they are attempting to lure the unsuspecting traveler with fares that are only accessible by Orbitz and their individual airline websites. The Department of Transportation has been investigating Orbitz for anticompetitive activities. Orbitz may have sold airfares that are not available through travel agent computer systems, Expedia, Travelocity or other travel search engines.

While I was researching, I found one instance where the fare was ONLY offered on Orbitz and not on their individual airline websites. Several days later the discount "web-only" airfare was added to the airline websites and the travel agency computers. That gave Orbitz an unfair advantage.[1]

What scares me is the possibility of price collusion. The partners can allegedly agree on prices in secret and then offer them only on the Orbitz

[1] When I first checked JFK-Paris-JFK, the lowest fare was the "OrbitzSaver" fare. At the time of the search this price was not offered in SABRE or online at *sidestep.com, expedia.com* or *travelocity.com*. Several days later I discovered the same airfare in my GDS and in Sidestep with a "web" coding fare basis.

website. Currently their ploy is to train the general public into thinking their site gives the best prices. Maybe today it does. But after you are hooked on using their site exclusively, they can secretly raise airfares above the rates of competing sites. To keep them in check, use *Sidestep.com* and their comparison search function. Any web-only airfare should be found using *Sidestep.com.* Orbitz is now charging a $5.00 per ticket service fee.

Qixo.com

A slow website for the truly price conscious.
QIXO.com is another comparison search engine like *Sidestep.com.* Besides the airlines, hotels and car vendors QIXO searches websites of wholesalers and other travel agency search engines. It's possible that you might turn up an itinerary for $10 less, but this website takes an eternity to respond. My searches took several minutes at best. I got the same responses on *Sidestep.com* in seconds. What they do have is "QIXbot," a search program that watches your chosen itinerary for several hours in case a cheaper fare appears prior to purchase.

Travelocity.com

1-888-709-5973
I am continuously disappointed in this website. They are slowly becoming user-friendly but still have adjustments to make. You can now search itineraries but cannot see the pricing details until you log-on.

Go to the "advanced flight search" to have better control over your guidelines. Once you fill in the availability search boxes the site usually defaults to a window with a "featured airline" suggestion. This is really *covert advertising.*

When you get your response it will be based on a roundtrip itinerary, a key disadvantage. If you want one flight from one combination and one from another, it is extremely difficult to get the system to bypass their own selections.

But it does have good points. It gives flight choices that are closer to your requested guidelines and has most of the available discounted fares. They also negotiate special discount fares with the various airlines and offer them as "web fares." If you don't mind the log-in, roundtrip choices, and covert advertising, you might find it is a decent website to use.

Travel Agency Computer Systems

The GDS, Global Distribution System, also called CRS, Computer Reservation System, used by travel agencies are some of the same computers used by the travel search engines but with different and more specific search criteria. A travel agent that is fully trained in the use of her/his GDS can, most of the time, quickly come up with the same fares you get (except web-only fares), or possibly lower ones on alternate flights. See the explanation of a travel agent's computer screen in Chapter 8.2, *Anatomy of an Airfare.*

The human touch can also offer options like an alternate airport. A travel agent can check the availability of a flight directly with that airline's database to see if there is a seat or two available for a cheaper fare. The search is relatively quick depending on how sold out your dates are. A travel agent will be familiar with the rules of the airfares and can suggest different days or flights for a lower airfare. Few travel search engines will offer you alternatives. There are simply too many, and *you need human intervention* to narrow down your choices. But, alas, there is that pesky old service fee that travel agents have to charge so they can stay in business. This nominal service fee is well worth the price.

A travel agent will also be aware of problems with the airlines. You may feel the price is most important but a travel agent may be able to warn you if there is something fishy about an airline or destination. Are there threats of strikes, financial difficulties or maintenance violations? Has the U.S. issued a travel warning?

Bidding for Airline Tickets

An interesting note, an article in one of my trade papers, *Travel Weekly,*[2] stated that in their early days of operation *priceline.com* said a large percentage of the tickets purchased were regular nonrefundable airfares that could have been purchased anywhere. This is still the case. This indicates that the average ticket purchaser does not know the cost of an airline ticket and is bidding blindly. How do you know what amount to bid if you haven't checked out the prices elsewhere?

---

[2] *Travel Weekly,* November 22, 1999.

Most people turn to *priceline.com* when they have planned their trip too late to get reasonable prices directly from the airline or travel agent. Or, more often than not, they are caught up in the frenzy to surf the web for bargains.

Priceline.com has changed their strategy and improved their website dramatically. You now have better control with the new guidelines. You can now chose whether or not you can fly at off peak travel times, make up to 2 connections or fly on a propeller aircraft. And they now have limited the airline choices to the MAJOR "full service" airlines. Oddball connections and long travel times were major drawbacks for them. Hopefully, the new guidelines will alleviate some of that problem.

Also try *expedia.com*'s website for "FLIGHT PRICE MATCHER" for another bidding program.

How to Bid for Airline Tickets

1. Check with *Sidestep.com* and/or *expedia.com* for today's going rate of an airline ticket for your cities.
2. Determine how much you want to pay for your airline ticket. Include:
   —*priceline.com*'s $5.95 ticket processing fee
   —Government "taxes" of approximately $40
   —Add the above to the price you want to pay for your airline ticket to get the amount you will BID.
3. BID. Fill in the screens, read all information, guidelines and suggestions.
4. Give your credit card and personal information. Look over the fill-in form for accuracy. Once you submit your bid, you are committed to the purchase. You cannot change it, refund it or give it to someone else. You are not eligible for frequent flyer miles.
5. Wait for the email reply.

Handicaps of Using the Web

- You need to know how to use a computer and the Web to do comparison-shopping.
- The airlines may not notify you of schedule changes if you book online.
- You can spend hours searching. If you have spent 5 hours searching the Web for the best airfare to save $50, is it a valuable use of your time?

- The Web can't offer you alternatives like a human being can. If you live in Washington, DC, the Web most likely won't suggest that you fly out of nearby Baltimore Airport and save possibly 50% on your airfare.
- A travel agent, and sometimes an agent at an airline, can suggest you fly at a different time, or date, or make a connecting flight to save money. A travel site might advise you to do this but does not show you when and how.
- Sometimes you need the assurance of a human being. Someone you can ask a question and get an answer.
- An agent will tell you the rules and penalties attached to the ticket you are purchasing. On a travel website, you have to seek out this information, which is commonly written in airline lingo. If you don't look up the rules of the fare, you may run into trouble when you try to change it.

Tips for Surfing the Web

- Load *sidestep.com* onto your browser for their comparison search.
- Have your travel guidelines ready.
- As with any travel search, use the information gathered as a starting point in your research.
- It is recommended that you only book one airline for your entire trip.
- Pay by credit card, not a debit/ATM card or check or cash.
- Purchase your ticket within 60 days of travel to be eligible for credit card protection.

Have lots of time and patience to do your search. Last minute or being in a rush could cost you money.

CHAPTER 8.4

Sources for Airline Discounts

Finding airline discounts is simpler than you think, especially if you know where to look. Here are a few I have found and have worked with, listed alphabetically.

AARP: The American Association of Retired Persons: anyone over 50 can join for a fee of $12.50 per year. Discounts vary, some are 10% off, other airfares are negotiated rates. Ask for the lowest fare available. *Sidestep.com* has a profile window where you can indicate that you are eligible for an AARP discount.

Alternate Cities: Certain cities, especially those that have a "no frills" airline flying into them, will have cheaper airfares. If a "no frills" airline flies into an airport within a reasonable driving distance, you may want to consider this as an alternative. Check both the "no frills" airline and any competing major airline that fly into this same airport. Usually they charge the same airfare.

Back-to-Back Ticketing: These are two roundtrip nonrefundable tickets that you either use only the first leg/flight coupon from each ticket or you use all the coupons but "out of date order."

Although this is not illegal, the major airlines make a determined effort to prohibit this practice by going after any travel agent that issues them. They also look at your frequent flyer statements. This practice was so common that the airlines wrote new software programs to catch people doing this. They primarily went after the travel agents who are easier to police (by charging them the full price of the tickets). Then

they started looking at the frequent flyer statements. The airlines claim they will stop you at check-in and demand the additional money due.

For example: What if you have to fly from JFK to San Francisco on Monday and back on Friday of the same week. You need to do this, two weeks in a row. Without a Saturday night stay, your airfare for each ticket will be over $2200 roundtrip, approximately $4400 for both. A way around this is to buy two roundtrip nonrefundable tickets, on *DIFFERENT AIRLINES*, approximately $356.50 each, a total of $713, and use all the flight coupons, but out of date sequence. The date sequence is the key. Here is an example:

Ticket 1:

1.	Depart:	Monday	Aug 05	JFK-SFO
2.	Return:	2nd Friday	Aug 16	SFO-JFK

Ticket 2:

3.	Depart:	1st Friday	Aug 09	SFO-JFK
4.	Return:	2nd Monday	Aug 12	JFK-SFO

You will carry both tickets with you on both trips and use the coupons listed, in this order: 1 and 3, then 4 and 2.

You will be using all the flight coupons but, according to airline thinking, out of date sequence. They think if you travel on Monday and return on Friday of the same week, you should buy a ticket written that way and pay the higher price: $2200.

The secret here is to buy the two nonrefundable tickets on *DIFFERENT AIRLINES*, i.e., one on United and the other on American, not two on United or two on American. Or you can fly into Oakland, CA, buy two nonrefundable tickets on jetBlue, who does not care if you do this, AND save an additional $80!

Another scheme people use if they are not staying over a Saturday night and only traveling Monday to Friday once, is to buy two tickets and only use the first flight coupon of each ticket, discarding the other coupon when your trip is completed. But it is cheaper to buy one roundtrip non-refundable ticket from a "no frills" airline and avoid the major airline hassle.

This is a very gray legal issue and is best to avoid it, if possible. There are enough "no frill" airlines out there flying to San Francisco that you can avoid the big guy's pressure tactics altogether. The only reason to fly the big guys is if you are fanatically collecting frequent flyer miles.

Bereavement Fares/Emergency Travel: included here as information only. It is NOT a standard way of getting a discount. But, everyone, at some point, loses someone close to them. You don't want added headaches when you are making funeral arrangements. If you need to fly to an immediate family member's funeral, the airlines offer special bereavement fares: a discounted fare of some sort. The rules and discounts vary by airline. Call several airlines and compare or call a travel agent who knows which airline will give you the best discount. (These special fares are not offered online.) All the airlines require proof that you are attending a funeral. You will need to supply the name of the deceased, your relationship to them, name of funeral home, and phone number. They check the information you give, so don't try to use this as a ploy to get a last-minute discount.

Bidding or Name Your Own Price: Companies such as *priceline.com* or *expedia.com* have bidding programs. From another source, verify the best discount you can get for your travel dates. Then put in a bid. Be sure you have read and understand the rules. See the section, Bidding For Airline Tickets in Chapter 8.3, *Surf the Web for Airfares* for guidelines.

Charters: There still are a few around. Savvy wholesalers who see a need, charter an aircraft to transport a group of people to a holiday or an ethnic destination. Usually your payment goes into a bank escrow account that is cashed after you have traveled. Your chance of losing your money is high, so check out the organizer's financial connections, how long they've been in business, what is their sales volume, and how much profit have they made in the past 5 years. Listen to your gut instinct (or your spouse) and don't get caught up in hyped sales talk.

Companion Tickets: The most common one of these is the American Express Platinum Card promotion: buy one full-price business class fare, get a second one "FREE." If you can fit into their HIGHLY RESTRICTIVE guidelines, i.e., only certain airlines, specific routings, blackout dates, advance purchase, etc., you can save thousands of dollars. You now have to do this yourself or pay a high service fee to a travel agent. American Express now charges the travel agent a service fee for an authorization code. If the travel agent makes a mistake or does not get this code, they are responsible for the full value of the ticket.

Also, check for credit card promos or coupons in entertainment guides. They sometimes offer a companion free coupon, or a $100 discount or some other amount.

Connecting Cities: If you are traveling anywhere near Las Vegas or Orlando, compare the price of your selected routing to one that *connects* via either Las Vegas or Orlando. The demand in these markets creates lower airfares. This also applies if your original flight is nonstop. Try a connection—it might be cheaper.

Consolidators: are companies that negotiate discounted (usually international) airfares or buy seats in bulk from the airlines. The rates can be cheaper than tickets bought through the airlines when the airlines are *NOT* having a seasonal sale. Before you book with a consolidator, check elsewhere for the current rates. Check online at the airline websites and with a travel search engine such as *expedia.com* or *travelocity.com.* If you're not a computer user, call a travel agent or the airlines directly. Again, the travel agent will charge you a service fee.

Often consolidator tickets cost more than those bought through other sources and are more restrictive. Best to check around before giving your credit card number. Some restrictions might be:

- No frequent flyer miles.
- Nonrefundable/non-changeable.
- May be able to change return only, for an airline imposed $200 fee plus any fee levied by the consolidator.
- Rarely can change the outbound flight without heavy penalties.
- Limited seat availability.
- ***Potentially financially unstable business—you could lose investment. Only use reputable ones and pay by credit card within 60 days of departure.***
- Schedules tend to be inconvenient.
- Tickets are not transferable to another airline if there is a problem with your flight, if it is delayed, or the airline goes out of business. The airline does not have to provide you with any delay compensation in the form of a free meal or overnight hotel. You could end up waiting until the next day to travel.
- No advance seat assignments. You can only get them at check-in on departure. You could end up with a middle seat.

- You cannot request a special meal even if it is a diet-restricted meal.
- They do not offer senior discounts or any other discounts.
- Your ticket is nonrefundable and is governed by the standard nonrefundable tariff rulings of your fare.

Points to Note

- Check with the airline first to compare airfare.
- Pay by credit card within 60 days of departure for your financial protection.
- Get a written confirmation with the airline record locator and proof of your electronic ticket (passenger receipt), or the actual ticket, within 7 days of payment.
- Call the airline you are ticketed on and verify that you do have a reservation. Book seats if they allow it.

Travel agents are required to advise you that these tickets are highly restrictive and that they can be sued for nondisclosure.

Credit Card Programs: Various promotions exist. Call and ask both the airline and your credit card company if they have partner frequent flyer programs. More than 50% of all frequent flyer miles are collected on the ground, not from flying. Often when you open a frequent flyer credit card, they offer a free companion ticket coupon, discount coupon, or bonus miles. Beware that the interest rate on these cards is very high if you carry a balance.

Entertainment Guides: These books are offered only in certain markets and can usually be purchased in your local bookstore. Some of the guides contain a Continental Airlines coupon for a free companion ticket. They also contain hotel discounts. Check the book for discounts before you buy it.

"Fare Wars"

Twice a year the airlines run a *major sale* offering deeply discounted fares. These fares tend to be less expensive than the regular nonrefundable discounted airfares. At one time these were called "fare wars" where the other airlines would match the fares. Now they call them "sales." The airlines advertise the "sales" heavily, just like the department store in your local mall. If you have the Internet, sign up for one or two airline's weekly email newsletters. Usually they advise you of a "sale." During the past several years these sales have been run:

For Domestic Flights:

- Mid-December through the end of January
- Mid-July through mid-August

The sales are usually run for a short period of time, generally for 3–5 days. Then they bring in a new "sale" with an increase in the rate, sometimes $30, and extend the "sale" dates. This is repeated in 3–5 day increments for several weeks.

Along with the sale date window is the list of weeks that travel is valid. The first sale could be valid for traveling in the month of January; the next sale adds the month of February, and so on. The premise here is to fill the airline's pocketbook when travel is slow. If the airlines are having a great season, they will limit the sales.

For International Fares:

- Mid-December through the end of March, especially for European flights.

The earlier you book, the cheaper the fare. If you wait until the end of March to buy your summer ticket, you will probably find that most of the nonrefundable seats to Europe are already sold out.

- Winter travel, low season, to Europe is considerably cheaper than high season, summer.

AUTHOR'S NOTE

Buy a nonrefundable "sale" ticket to Europe and travel during the less expensive winter months. For around $400, you can collect approximately 7,000 frequent flyer miles.

Buying your ticket during sale season is the most common and simplest way to get the best discount fare through normal sources: airlines, travel agents or online. If you plan around these sales, you could save another 25%.

Frequent Flyer Programs: This is the most common way to get discounts in the form of free tickets or upgrades. See Chapter 15 for explanation. Each airline program is different, so check the rules. Plan 11 months in advance if traveling over peak holiday time or in the summer to Europe. To get the best value for your miles, buy an economy ticket—sometimes a nonrefundable fare is allowed—and upgrade to the next class, either business or first. Don't waste 25,000 frequent flyer miles for a free ticket in a market with a $250 nonrefundable airfare. Instead, splurge—use 30,000 miles, buy a $1,200 ticket (or less) and upgrade to business class, saving over $3,000! This is a better use of your hard-earned miles.

Most frequent flyer programs no longer expire if there is some sort of activity on the account. This includes miles earned from a credit card. Get an airline mileage credit card to make all your purchases. But beware of the very high interest rate if you carry a balance.

Getting Bumped: The airlines are experts on load factors but sometimes weather, miscellaneous circumstances or too many people showing up for the same flight can cause a miscalculation. When this happens, the airline will ask for volunteers to give up their seats in exchange for a transportation voucher. The amount is negotiable depending on how desperately they need your seat. You will be put on the next available flight, sometimes in first class, and get the voucher. You can almost make a career out of this. If you can find the heavily booked flights, you can get bumped and travel this way all the time. NOTE: transportation vouchers are not replaceable so don't lose them. Also, you must redeem them in person. You cannot use them as payment for tickets purchased online.

Internet Latesaver Fares, Domestic: These fares can be purchased only through the web. Most airlines offer special discounts that are announced to their email customers. Promotional fares usually come out on Wednesdays for travel the following weekend. This has been expanded to offer other promos. These are used to fill up unsold seats for off-peak travel.

Travel via Las Vegas: If you make a connection (take 2 flights instead of one) through Las Vegas, you can take advantage of the two-day minimum stay requirement on nonrefundable airfares, instead of the Saturday night stay of other cities. This will work for any two cities that have Las Vegas in between.

"No Frills" Airlines: These are the newer airlines that offer few services to keep airfares low. The FAA keeps a tight watch over them. The lower fares create competition and keep fares in their markets low. Unfair marketing tactics from the big guys make it hard for the "no frills" airlines to stay in business. Usually they sell one-way fares at a deep discount, with capacity controlled inventories. Some of these airlines tend to be financially unstable so it is wise to use a credit card to pay for your ticket within 60 days of travel.

Nonrefundable Fares

Ongoing Discounts, Fares Vary: These are your standard economy class discounted fares. More than likely, this is the type of ticket you will purchase. In general, if the price of your domestic airline ticket is less than $750, you have probably bought a restricted nonrefundable ticket. Always ask what the rules are and write them down with the requirements and minimum stay. You can purchase your ticket from the airline, travel agent or via the Internet. See detailed rules and explanation in Chapter 8.2, *Anatomy of an Airfare.*

STANDARD RULES, most will apply:

- **Advance purchase required.** Could be 3, 7, 10, 14, 21, or 30 days prior to departure date.
- In most markets, you must purchase a **roundtrip** ticket to get this special fare. Certain markets, such as Las Vegas and Orlando, have one-way nonrefundable fares.
- **Ticket is valid only** on the flight and date shown. Has no value if you don't show up for your flight or neglect to change it prior to the dates on the ticket.
- Normally has a **minimum stay** of one Saturday night (Las Vegas has a 2-day).

- Normally has a 30-day **maximum stay** but can vary depending on market and airfare.
- Must "**purchase within 24 hours** of reservation" (by midnight of the next day) or by the 7, 14, 21 days advanced purchase rule, whichever comes first.
- Has a **penalty fee** of $100 if you change it. If your new airfare is more than the old one, you will also have to pay the additional airfare.
- You **get frequent flyer miles**, depending on where you purchased your ticket.
- Seat assignments, if applicable.
- Special dietary meals, if applicable, and if requested in advance on a flight that serves a meal.
- **Capacity controlled inventory.**

Partner Promos: Airlines make promotional agreements with every possible retail entity. Call your favorite airline and ask them to look up the list of promotions they have going. Then run and buy the 400 cans of tuna fish to get that free ticket! Some may be useful, so call and ask. Any discount coupon you get from any source is usually highly restricted, with blackout dates and capacity controlled inventories. You'll have to avoid peak travel dates (school vacation weeks). The coupon is most likely not going to be valid. Then what will you do with all that tuna fish?

Split Ticketing–International Travel: If you are buying an unrestricted INTERNATIONAL airfare (First, Business, or Full fare economy class) compare the rate of a roundtrip ticket to two separate one-way tickets, one in U.S. Dollars when you originate in the U.S. and one in the foreign currency of the country you are returning from. This is especially true for countries with a weak economy. If you fly Los Angeles to Hong Kong, in business class, you can save approx $550 just by buying two separate tickets instead of one roundtrip ticket.

LAX to HKG: could cost $3,087.70
HKG to LAX: could cost $2,521.60
Total for 2 separate tkts $5,609.30
Roundtrip fare: $6,199.30 if one ticket purchased
Savings: $590

The airlines became aware of the split-ticketing scheme and have added a special discounted roundtrip airfare if you fly to certain countries on the same airline. Also, compare the prices among the airlines. Sometimes one airline is cheaper than another.

Split Pricing–Domestic Travel: On rare occasions, comparing the total roundtrip fare of an itinerary to the individual segment prices can work out cheaper. I am always puzzled when I see this. It is a unique occurrence but does happen, usually in markets that have discount airlines creating competition. When the computer prices your ticket, it considers several guidelines from the information of the *first flight*, mainly the departure date. The GDS will miss any special fares that are valid for originating elsewhere and on different dates. If you are connecting along the way, definitely compare the airfares to and from the connecting city. It takes time doing this and would probably not even be possible using the Internet. Try a travel agent. It's faster and could save you hundreds of dollars.

Student/Youth Fares–International: These fares are offered only in international markets and are for legitimate students ages 12 to 24 with school identification and valid passport. These fares are not offered in all markets. You must make your reservation and buy your ticket at the same time but within 72 hours of departure. You can have an open return but must book your flight also within 72 hours of departure. These tickets are nonrefundable and subject to holiday blackouts. You cannot change the outbound flight once you have purchased your ticket: "use it or lose it."

Senior Discounts: This is another discount removed by many of the major airlines as a cost-cutting measure. Verify with your airline as to the senior discount they may offer. US Airways has a "zone" contract fare with AARP. Other airlines may offer coupon booklets.

Senior Coupons Booklets: Many airlines have phased these out. The airlines assume you are retired and can travel at any time so they have added "blackout periods" which restrict the time of day and date you can travel. You must be 62 or older to use these nonrefundable tickets. You buy a coupon booklet from the airline or travel agent and then redeem it for the actual nonrefundable ticket in advance. The booklets are sold with 4 or 8 coupons and can be used for one-way or roundtrip travel. Reservations must be made more than 14 days in advance. If you book less than 14 days in advance you may be able to standby. As with other nonrefundable tickets, the seats are limited.

Web-Only Airfares: These are discounted airfares offered for sale only online at airline websites or airline owned travel search engines such as *orbitz.com.* Other travel search engines not owned by the airlines, such as *expedia.com* have also been able to negotiate discount airfares and call them web fares. Eventually the other airline ticket websites will negotiate these web discount fares.

CHAPTER 8.5

How to Make an Airline Reservation

Review Established Guidelines

You are probably tired of me reminding you to have your guidelines established. Get out your filled in PREPLANNING SUMMARY SHEET. Let's review:

1. **The Travelers:** Whom are you traveling with? The names, ages and any frequent flyer numbers should be on the sheet.
2. **Timing:** When are you going? Now is the time to be specific. Write the dates you want to travel. Also note how flexible you are. Can you travel a day earlier or later?
3. **Activities:** Make note of any activities that need to be prearranged and that may have a bearing on your travel dates, such as attending a conference or concert.
4. **Destination:** You know where you want to go. But are you aware of another airport within reasonable driving distance that might bring the cost of the airfare down considerably?
5. **Budget:** Have your valid credit card ready. Write the number on the sheet. Will you use one card for the airline tickets and another for the hotel or car rental?
6. **Mode of Transportation:** If you are reading this chapter, you are probably flying!

Research

Once you have a general idea of your destination and activities, you can start your research. See Chapter 7, *Research You Must Do*, for help. Surf the web (See Chapter 8) or call a travel agent for help (See Chapter 12). Chose the airline, dates and flights along with your preferred hotel. Before booking and paying for either, be sure your choices are available at the rate you prefer. Also decide if you will purchase the components separately or all together in a package.

Choosing a Booking Source

By this time, you have done your research, looked online, browsed bookstores or spoken to a travel agent. You should have a general idea how much your airline ticket will cost and what the availability looks like. You should also have researched where you want to stay and have a few hotel names selected. Now you need to decide which booking source you will use.

Online: If you are confident that your research has found the best airfare and routing and you found a hotel that is reasonably priced and well located, you may want to go online to a travel search engine and book each part of the trip separately.

By Phone: The procedure is the same as online booking above except you call the toll-free numbers of the various vendors.

Call a Travel Agent: With notes and guidelines in hand, call a travel agent to help you book your trip. You can find a travel agent by looking through Chapter 12.1, *How to Find a Reliable Travel Agent*. Discuss with the travel agent whether or not to buy a package that includes your air and hotel.

Book It

See Figure 8.5 for the *AIRLINE RESERVATION SHEET*. Use this sheet to record your airline flight information. Note the travelers' names, ages and frequent flyer numbers. Then write down the flight information. Note the names of the airports, departure and arrival times. If you are connecting, also write down those times. You may need to know how much time on the ground you have when you are between flights. There is a space for noting your seat numbers and any special requests you might have, i.e., wheelchairs. *PLEASE, PLEASE NOTE THE RULES OF YOUR AIRFARE. PAY CLOSE ATTENTION TO THE CHANGE/PENALTY FEE.* When you have completed making your reservation, note the confirmation number. You will need this number to check in at the airport.

Write Information Down

It is essential that you either use the AIRLINE RESERVATION SHEET (Figure 8.5) or a piece of paper to note your reservation information. Whatever source you use, you still need to write down what has been confirmed when you make your reservation. Quite often what you thought you booked is different from what was actually confirmed. You or the travel agent may have made a typo when inputting the date, or you were not paying attention when the reservation was read back to you. You need a written sheet to compare to the confirmation you will get from the airline, website or travel agent. If a mistake has been made, you need to correct it immediately.

Proofread Your Written Confirmation

After you have purchased your airline ticket, you should receive an itinerary either emailed, faxed or snail mailed. *IMMEDIATELY LOOK OVER FOR ACCURACY.* Compare the itinerary with your written notes. Pay particular attention to the spelling of names and all dates. If you find any errors, don't panic. Immediately go back to the source and get it fixed. This should be done within 24 hours of original booking. If you booked online, you must call the airline directly and may have to pay a penalty fee to fix your mistake.

I CANNOT SAY THIS ENOUGH:
READ YOUR ITINERARY IMMEDIATELY FOR ACCURACY.
THEN HAVE YOUR TRAVELING COMPANION READ IT!

Make a note of the cancellation policies for the airline ticket and hotel reservations.

Airline Reservation Sheet

FIGURE 8.5

Date ____________

THE TRAVELERS:

____________ Age ______ Freq Flyer # ____________
____________ Age ______ Freq Flyer # ____________
____________ Age ______ Freq Flyer # ____________
____________ Age ______ Freq Flyer # ____________

Memberships: AAA # ____________ AARP # ____________

OUTBOUND FLIGHT INFORMATION

Date: ________ Day ________
Airline ________ Flight # ________
From ________ Time ________
Arr.Arpt. ________ Time ________
If Conx A/L ________ Flight # ________
Dptr. Arpt. ________ Time ________
Arr.Arpt. ________ Time ________
Seat Numbers: Out: ____________
Special Requests: ____________
Airfare: Per Adult: ____________
Rules: (Advance Purchase By,Nonref, Penalty Fee, etc.)
Confirmation Number: ____________

RETURN FLIGHT INFORMATION

Date: ________ Day ________
Airline ________ Flight # ________
From ________ Time ________
Arr.Arpt. ________ Time ________
If Conx A/L ________ Flight # ________
Dptr. Arpt. ________ Time ________
Arr.Arpt. ________ Time ________
Return: ____________
Other: ____________

Booking Source: ____________

Credit Card # ____________ Exp. Date ________
Cardholder Name ____________ Code on Card ________
Total Amount Charged ____________ Date Charged ________

Part Four: How To's for Hotels

Chapter 9	Overview of Hotels	113
Chapter 9.1	What Is Included in the Room Rate	123
Chapter 9.2	Determining Your Basic Hotel Needs	128
Chapter 9.3	Hotel Research	130
Chapter 9.4	Surf the Web for Hotels	140
Chapter 9.5	Sources for Hotel Discounts	147

CHAPTER 9

Overview of Hotels

AUTHOR'S NOTE

The term "hotel" is used throughout this book as a general term referring to where you sleep at night. When you research your "hotel" information, you may choose to stay at a property that is called something other than "hotel."

Probably the most costly portion of your trip will be your hotel. Your airline ticket may only cost as much as one night of your hotel stay. First you need to separate your wish list/desires from your actual needs. Then you will be able to select a hotel that will fit your needs based on what you want to do on vacation and how much you want to spend.

Besides availability, there is an infinite list of items that can affect the price of your hotel room.

Types of Hotels

A hotel is something more than a building with a bed. "Hotels" around the world vary considerably in description and services. Following is a brief explanation of the types of hotels.

Hotel: This is a generic term for a number of rooms offered for sale by someone wanting to make money. A hotel's size can vary from two rooms to thousands of rooms. There is a wide variation in what the hotel offers in services and the rate it charges.

Motel: This is a word derived from "motor"—as in automobile and "hotel": MOtor-hoTEL. Generally motels are smaller in size and have only a few floors with stairs instead of elevators. Traditionally there are no inside hallways, and all rooms open to the outdoors. Few amenities are offered besides free parking. Often they do not have a restaurant on site.

Resort: This type of hotel offers so many features/services that you won't need to venture off the property for anything you need. They might have shops, several restaurants, a view of some sort, possibly a spa, and activities. Generally, you pay for any service you use, pay as you go.

All-Inclusive: This is a resort-type hotel that generally includes most food, drinks and "toys" in the cost of your room.

Suite Hotel, Condo, or Apartment: These properties generally have a kitchenette, dining area, living room area, and sleeping area, possibly in one large room. Sometimes a complimentary continental breakfast is included in the rate. Housekeeping services vary, so ask when booking. These properties range from cheap dumps to deluxe, family-oriented accommodations.

Boutique Hotel: These are small hotels in large cities. Someone with flair and imagination designs the property in a way that this is its lure. They may or may not have a restaurant or the amenities of a full service hotel.

Bed and Breakfast Hotel: Generally someone's former home. Too big and too expensive to live in, so the owner turned it into a business, decorated with imagination and opened to the public. Home-cooked breakfast is usually included. Sometimes small inns are considered B & Bs. Contrary to general belief, these are usually on the expensive side.

Anything with a Roof and a Bed: This could be a tent, a cabin or underwater bubble—with and without critters.

The hotel rating system around the world varies depending on the advertising spin of management and the government rating system, if there is one.

Quality of Your Hotel

The "star" rating or category of a hotel in the U.S. can be difficult to determine. Hotel standards are strictly arbitrary. *THERE IS NO GOVERNING AGENCY IN THE UNITED STATES OR CANADA THAT CONTROLS THESE STANDARDS.* The marketing manager/owner of a hotel determines what category his hotel fits in. A new hotel might be initially categorized as a deluxe hotel, but after 5 years of neglect may no longer be considered deluxe by the general public. However, it might still be advertised and priced as deluxe. It is difficult to determine the quality of a hotel from a website, hotel brochure, or tourist board listing.

FOR EXAMPLE: I recently stayed in a hotel in Massachusetts that was considered a "resort" hotel. It was on a marina, had a pool, and offered a continental breakfast with store-bought donuts. The property was not maintained. The mold and mildew in the bathroom went completely up the tiled wall, across the ceiling and out the bathroom door into the hallway. Wet towels hung on the doorway hook caused mildew to the unpainted wood beneath them. The unpainted balcony wood had a coating of green mildew all over it. Real creepy place.

To my knowledge, this property is not listed in any travel guide of note, but does have a listing on the town's travel website. Unsuspecting travelers will be surprised when they get there. Also, the hotel has the word "resort" in its name, a term perceived to mean an upscale property. In this case it is extremely misleading.

About 10 years ago I stayed at a hotel that was then a member of the Hilton hotel chain, usually considered a first class and above hotel category. This hotel had indoor/outdoor carpeting in the lobby, as well as a Formica sink top in my room that was partially pulled off. This property is no longer a Hilton. Hilton has since recategorized their properties to separate the truly deluxe ones, such as the Waldorf Astoria in New York City, from the "not deluxe" properties now considered Hilton Garden Inns. This seems to be a trend throughout the hotel industry.

AUTHOR'S NOTE

Doing research online can only give you the marketing spin and not the true "feel" of a hotel. This is where you need to speak to a travel agent that has experience with your destination. Friends that have been there are speaking from their perspective, which could be different from yours. Tourist boards cannot give opinions about a property. They must remain impartial.

Determining the True Quality of a Hotel

In the U.S., the way you can guarantee the quality of a hotel is to stay at a chain hotel or a hotel that is a member of a hotel organization with quality standards, such as Leading Hotels of the World. Chains like Days Inn and Microtel have their own rating standards that the member hotels must subscribe to. Other inexpensive hotels may or may not have a minimum standard nor have a way to police these properties. The quality of the hotels may vary considerably within the economic hotel chains.

An independent hotel, one that does not belong to a chain or an association like Triple A (AAA), may be impossible to judge from printed sources or websites. If the hotel is any good, magazines like *Condé Nast Traveler* or *Travel and Leisure* may write about them. The hotel would then have bragging rights. Be wary of any hotel whose quality cannot be verified in some way.

Keep in mind:

**ECONOMIC RULE OF THUMB:
YOU GET WHAT YOU PAY FOR**

For hotels around the world, a good source book is the Michelin Red book, but they don't publish one for every country.

Chain Hotels

What is a chain hotel? It is a member of a group of hotels managed by a larger hotel company. They carry the same name, MUST adhere to company policy regarding hotel maintenance, staff performance, and share the same reservation system. Examples are Hyatt, Hilton, and Days Inn. You can depend on getting the same quality of service and accommodations at each of the chain's hotels. This consistency is important in maintaining the chain's image. Many hotel corporations have different rating levels of hotel chains in order to not dilute the category standards of each brand. For instance, the Marriott Corporation has deluxe Marriott Hotels, moderate Courtyard Hotels, and economy Fairfield Inns. You will not find an economy rated hotel that's called a Marriott.

Generic Hotel Rating System

Since there is no official hotel rating system, I will give you mine. It is a cross section from AAA, Expedia and other travel sources. You may not agree—use as a guideline only.

Luxury: Top-of-the-line hotel providing total pampering. Whatever you want, you get and pay dearly for it.

Super Deluxe: Luxury wannabes. These hotels tend to be larger, may be part of an upscale chain, but fall short of total pampering. They may be overpriced for their value.

Deluxe: Traditionally, these cater to business travelers and are hotels located in big city central locations. They have a well-trained concierge staff that can handle special services such as obtaining theatre tickets.

First Class: Somewhere between deluxe and moderate. These do not provide much service but are located in busy areas that justify the higher rate. They may have several restaurants, a business center, or a fitness center.

Moderate: Budget-minded business traveler category. They may have a restaurant, fitness center and free weekday newspapers. Generally, they are unable to provide any special services.

Inexpensive: Hopefully a clean bed and bathroom. Unpredictable category.

Dump: Lumpy beds, nonexistent service, lousy location, and you may have to share with nonpaying critters.

See the Appendix for a hotel list including my ratings, phone numbers and websites.

Why Do Rates Vary?

There are many reasons. There may be a hotel somewhere that charges the same rate for every room every night of the year, but normally the room rate is subject to the supply and demand concept of economics. The more popular a room location or the more in demand a check-in date, the more they can get for the room. Sometimes the check-in date determines the per night rate of your stay, such as a higher rate if you check in on Saturday. Or, as in Las Vegas, the room rate can vary every night of your stay. Here is a list that affects the rate of a hotel room:

- **Season:** Peak season dates, such as school vacations and holidays. For example, Caribbean and ski destinations in the winter, Europe in the summer.
- **Special Events:** Superbowl, conventions, any activity that draws a large crowd will boost the rate.
- **Location of the Hotel:** The more desirable a location, the higher the price, i.e., beach front, on the ski slope, downtown, etc.
- **Location of the Room Within the Hotel:** An oceanfront room is going to bring top dollar compared to the least expensive room in the back near the delivery or garbage recycling area.
- **Availability:** Sophisticated yield management programs allow a hotel to manipulate the rates based on how many rooms have been sold in advance.

- **Hotel Quality and Services Provided:** The larger the number of staff providing special services, the higher the room rate.
- **The Number of People and Beds in a Room:** Often the room rate depends on the number of people occupying the room.

The better the room, the more in demand that room is, the higher the rate.

Hotel and Room Features

The amenities and features that a hotel provides have a great effect on the star rating of the property. The more special features, such as a business center, golf course, or gourmet restaurant, the higher the star rating and price of the room. Figure 9.0 has a list of common hotel and room features. Again, this is merely a guideline for selecting a hotel. The first-time traveler may not be aware of the options that are available.

FIGURE 9.0

Hotel Check Off List

1. BEDDING:

This is a critical part of your planning. If you have two adults, two children, and confirm a hotel room by price only, you could find your family of 4 in a noisy room with one single bed and the bathroom down the hall.

Number of People in Your Party ____________
Number of Beds You Will Need ____________
Number of Rooms You will Need ____________

A "need" is something that is essential to the quality of your life and you absolutely must have. A "want" is something you would like to have if you could afford it. Check off which is a need or a want. Chose your preferred bed type as a want.

Item	Need	Want
Nonsmoking room	____	____
Smoking room	____	____
King size bed	____	____
1 Queen bed	____	____
2 Queens	____	____
1 Double bed	____	____
2 Double beds	____	____
2 Twin beds	____	____
1 Twin bed	____	____

ROOM VIEW:

Item	Need	Want
Room with a view/general	____	____
Balcony	____	____
Terrace/lanai	____	____
Inside/courtyard	____	____
Street view	____	____
Pool view	____	____
Garden view	____	____
Mountain/lake view	____	____
Full Ocean Front	____	____
Partial ocean view	____	____
Quiet location	____	____
ROH/Run of the house	____	____
VIEW NOT IMPORTANT	____	____
OTHER	____	____

NOISE LEVEL

Item	Need	Want
Maximum quiet, unable to sleep with outside noise, prefer an inside room	____	____

SOME NOTES:
The name of the size of the bed varies depending on the country you are in. In Europe, a "twin" bed may actually be a smaller sized bed than Americans are used to. If you are a large person, this distinction is quite important. INTERPRETATION: Every hotel has its own name for their bedding. Sometimes a room listed as a double could have twin beds, double beds, single beds or queen beds. If your booking source does not specify the exact type of bedding, call the hotel and ask.

Item	Need	Want
Other bedding choices:		
1 European Single bed	_____	_____
2 European Single beds	_____	_____
3 European Single beds	_____	_____
A cot or rollaway	_____	_____
1 Crib	_____	_____
japanese matting	_____	_____
Sleeping bag	_____	_____

2. ROOM LOCATION:

Item	Need	Want
Elevator to floor	_____	_____
Walk up to floor	_____	_____
Baggage assistance	_____	_____
Some street noise ok	_____	_____
Noise level doesn't matter	_____	_____

Noisy locations of some rooms: facing street traffic, near pool, above disco, near bars or meeting rooms, near elevator or stairs, near ice machines, connecting rooms with children or rooms with partiers in them. You can try to prearrange a quiet room, but the hotel has little control over the noisy habits of your neighbors.

3. ROOM AMENITIES:
Let's assume the standard room has one bed, one bathroom with one sink, tub/shower, a closet, TV, table and chair. The less expensive your room, the more basic it will be. Your bathroom could be down the hall, or the toilet could be in the shower (where you can sit on the toilet and shower at the same time!)

Item	Need	Want
Double sinks	_____	_____
Shower separate area	_____	_____
Bidet	_____	_____
Bathtub	_____	_____
Bathroom in room	_____	_____
Bathroom down the hall	_____	_____

Hotel Check Off List (continued)

Item	Need	Want
Hairdryer	______	______
Couch/living room area	______	______
Table and chair	______	______
Desk and chair	______	______
Radio	______	______
Computer port/Internet	______	______
Reading lamps	______	______
Safe in the room	______	______
TV with cable stations	______	______
Refrigerator	______	______
Kitchenette	______	______
Telephone	______	______
Multiple telephones	______	______
Phone/ans machine	______	______
Air Conditioning	______	______
Adjoining rooms	______	______
Coffeemaker	______	______
Other	______	______
Other	______	______

4. TYPE OF ROOM

Item	Need	Want
Regular hotel room	______	______
Connecting/adjoining rms	______	______
Parking in front of room	______	______
Suite/sitting room	______	______
Cottage	______	______
Villa	______	______
Condo	______	______
Time share	______	______
Private plunge pool room	______	______

CHAPTER 9.1

What Is Included in the Room Rate

Room Rates and Categories

In the United States and Canada, hotel rates are generally quoted as a per night rate, single or double occupancy, nothing included. At resorts and international properties, this is sometimes called the European Plan (EP).

Hotel room rates vary depending on location, size and view of the room, number of beds, size of beds, and what is included. When booking your room, it is imperative to ask the category and location of your room, size and number of beds, and what is included in the rate. The least expensive rate will NOT be for the best room category.

Types of Rates

ALL OF THESE RATES ARE ROOM RATE ONLY. You must add taxes and anything else mandatory or used.

Rack Rate: This is the "suggested retail price," or a rate category for the majority of rooms in a hotel. They offer the same amenities, view, location, size, etc. This is almost a fictitious rate, because you probably can get a cheaper rate category by asking. All discounted rates are based on a percentage off this rate.

Corporate: This is a negotiated rate specifically for business travelers. This discounted rate can be for a specific company or for anyone traveling on business.

ROH—Run of the House: This is a discounted negotiated rate usually with tour packages where the room category is assigned at check-in. You could get any room in the hotel, good or bad.

Group or Incentive Rates: You may see this, but cannot purchase it on your own. These apply to a group of rooms booked at the same time under one name.

Promotional: A limited availability discounted rate offered to generate business on slow-selling dates. It usually includes a feature such as breakfast or champagne.

- **EP:** European Plan: room only, no meals included
- **CB:** Continental breakfast included
- **BB:** Buffet breakfast included
- **MAP:** Modified American Plan—two meals a day included
- **AP:** American Plan—three meals a day
- **All-inclusive:** supposedly everything you do and eat is included in rate

When confirming a rate, ask what is included in your rate.

Per Night Rates vs. Prepaid Package Rate

If you buy a *prepaid package*, the rate is usually quoted as a per person rate based on a minimum number of nights, and *minimum two people in a room*. Usually, but not always, the hotel room tax is included, as well as another feature such as transfers from the airport to your hotel, or meals. A key point to keep in mind when buying a package is verifying the room category, i.e., standard or deluxe oceanfront, and the bed size, i.e., king or two double beds etc. If you buy a generic room type called ROH (run of the house), your room category/rate is based on availability at time of check-in. You could get stuck with the worst room in the hotel or the best. Unless you negotiate for a better one, you will be assigned the least valuable room available at the time.

A person traveling alone will pay a higher rate. It is usually the double rate less a small amount. If the single rate is $200 per night, the double rate for two people sharing the room could be $225.

It is important to understand the difference between a per night rate and a prepaid package rate. For example, for two people staying three nights at "The Pretty Hotel," the rate quoted is $100 per night, total $300, plus tax and other add-ons. If they buy a prepaid package, the rate could be quoted as $150 per person for three nights ($150 times 2 people, total $300)—the same value if nothing is included. But packages usually include the hotel tax or another feature. If this is the case, it is best to ask before giving your credit card, then the prepaid package rate is the better value.

How the rate is quoted depends on who has given you the quote. *Normally you are given a per night rate,* nothing included, when you make a reservation through these sources:

- Hotel directly
- Hotel's reservation center
- Hotel chain's online website
- Online travel websites like *Expedia.com* or *Sidestep.com*
- Your travel agent's GDS (computer).

Sometimes these same sources can offer you a package rate that includes a meal or some other feature. Except for some online hotel booking sources and peak holiday travel, these rates often do not require prepayment, but only a credit card number to hold the reservation. Again, ask or verify policy of your booking source. Also verify the cancellation policy. Packages tend to be more restrictive than normal.

When you book a prepaid package, you normally buy it from a travel agent who should explain in detail what you are buying and the cancellation and change rules. You could buy it from an online travel site, but that entails its own risks. The responsibility is on your shoulders to read ALL the fine print. Packages are highly restrictive and carry steep penalties, e.g., can be totally nonrefundable.

Those Extra Charges

The list of additional charges that can be added to your hotel bill is as great as your imagination. The hotel can, and does add charges for anything it can get away with. Many times these charges are tantamount to being scams. It's best to be aware upfront for which items you may be charged extra. Is the charge something that only this one hotel has? Then the charge could be negotiable or you'll stay elsewhere. But if all the hotels in the area are charging this extra amount, you may have no choice but to pay it. My favorite extra charge is the energy surcharge. Some states, such as California, who have an electricity shortage, have added an additional 3% to the room rate.

Obviously this is an incomplete list. When making your reservation, ask what additional charges will be added to your hotel bill. Many are mandatory but not included in the rate you are quoted.

Mandatory Charges

- State tax
- Local or city and/or resort tax
- Energy surcharges, air conditioning surcharge
- VAT—value added tax—usually international
- Service charge—this could be in lieu of tipping chambermaids, bellboys, etc. 15% seems standard
- Per person/per day occupancy tax
- Early check-out fee, depending on policy

Standard Charges Based on Usage

- Restaurants, shops
- Health center, exercise room, pool, sauna
- Business center
- Transportation—hotel shuttle, limos
- Parking fees—valet or self-parking
- Baggage handling
- Crib or rollaway bed
- Additional person
- Safe in room
- Refrigerator and/or microwave in room
- In room movies on demand

Other (Excessive) Extra Charges

- Telephone surcharges—can be very expensive. Read the plastic card by your telephone, i.e., $1.00 per local phone call. Long distance calls can be charged $4 each plus 50¢ per minute. Higher per-minute rate for international calls.

- Computer access ports—you pay dearly for the convenience.
- Faxes or FedEx sent or received.
- Room service plus 15% service and/or a delivery fee.
- In room minibars—outrageously priced for the convenience.

When you check out of the hotel, look at your bill closely. Question any charge you do not understand. Dispute any charge that seems excessive or erroneous. Additional charges should be posted somewhere. If they are not readily visible, you may be able to have the charge removed.

A Note about Tipping

If you have tipped the bellman, doorman, chambermaid, etc. as you used them, you may be able to dispute a general charge for baggage handling or a resort cleaning fee added to your bill. Better yet, when you check in, ask the clerk what the tipping policy is. At a resort property this is important.

CHAPTER 9.2
Determining Your Basic Hotel Needs

What will be the absolute minimum you will need for your stay to be comfortable? Once you have determined the minimum, you can start adding hotel features that may or may not increase the cost of your hotel room.

Determining Your Bare Bones Needs

1. **How Many People Are There in Your Party?**
2. **Bedding: How Many Beds Do You Need? What Size Bed Do You Need?** Will a double bed be large enough or must you have a king-size bed? Generally the larger the bed, and the number of beds in one room, the more expensive the room rate.
3. **How Many Bathrooms Do You Need?** Will you be able to take turns using the bathroom? Or are you a bathroom hog? Traditionally, there is one bathroom per room.
4. **How Many Rooms Do You Need?** For one person, this is usually one room. For two or more people, the number of rooms you need depends on the number of beds in the room and whether you want to share one bathroom and occupy the same space for the entire stay.

How Will You Use Your Hotel Room?

Is your hotel room simply a place to sleep and shower, or will you be spending the majority of your time in your room?

1. **Sleep and Shower:** If you only need your room for the basics, then it is unnecessary to spend a lot of money for your room. You probably want a comfortable bed and clean bathroom.
2. **Everything You Do Will Be at the Same Hotel:** You probably want a resort hotel with added amenities and room service. The more you want, the more you pay.
3. **Home Base, Plus Relaxing:** You will be visiting the area and will both use the room as a place to sleep and shower as well as relax, use the pool, and eat at their restaurants.
4. **You Need Extra Space:** If you are a large family, or like to spread your stuff all over, then you may want to consider a suite-type property.

What Will You Do on Vacation?

Will you play golf, ski, or visit Disney World? Each activity has a different bearing on your hotel. If you play golf, you may want a resort with a golf course; if you ski, you may want a ski in/ski out hotel or a condo down the street. Disney World has properties on-site and within miles of the parks. Will you have a rental car or use public transportation?

Hotel Location and Getting Around

Where your hotel is located is a major factor in the price of your room. If you want a hotel on a beach or in a resort area, you will truly pay for the convenience. A decent hotel will be costly. A cheap/dumpy hotel could be overpriced and a poor value. A chain hotel at the airport may be cheaper than one downtown or on a beach.

Also keep in mind how you will get to your hotel. Will you be renting a car and have it available for your use during your entire stay? You need to factor in the cost of parking. Parking rates can be excessive—up to $35 per day.

If you use some type of airport transfer to get to your hotel, how will you get around while you are there? Will you be able to walk everywhere, or will you have to rely on public transportation like buses? Taxis are generally expensive. This is one important point in selecting your hotel: *how will you get around if you don't have a car?*

CHAPTER 9.3
Hotel Research

How to Select a Hotel

From the previous section you have decided:

1. The number of beds and rooms you will need.
2. General location of hotel: beach, resort, airport, etc.
3. What kind of transportation you will need to get to your hotel and use while you're there: rental car, local ground transportation, or private limo. Is the price of parking an issue?
4. What will you do while on vacation—play golf, sightsee, or relax? Does the hotel have to provide these services?
5. Type of hotel: regular hotel, suite-type.
6. Quality of hotel: inexpensive, moderate, or deluxe.
7. Relative budget for entire trip, divided by the number of nights of your stay (minus the cost of airline tickets, food, etc.).

Once you have a general idea of what type of hotel, quality or category you want, and where it should be located, you can start researching hotels and pick several that fit your guidelines.

Sources for Hotel Research

There are many places you can go to get hotel information. But you need to go to trusted sources. Unfortunately, the Internet is commonly NOT the best source for information, especially for hotels. Creating a website is costly, and the hotels hire the best advertising people to design a product that will bring folks to their site and property. The truth is stretched, intimated, intentionally omitted or possibly grossly overstated: and you, the consumer, must guess what's true. Unfortunately, you may not find out until you get to the hotel.

When was the last time you booked a hotel from a picture of two sexy adults holding drinks with little umbrellas sitting in comfy lounge chairs on the beach? Especially when you are considered a plus-sized adult towing two screaming kids.

The best way to narrow down your hotel search is to go to a BOOKSTORE OR LIBRARY and look (you can buy too) through the numerous travel guides for your destination. Guidebooks have usually checked out the properties before they recommend them in their book. Often, they list properties under categories by dollar amount, location or class. As a travel agent, even I use these sources as a trusted resource. It is impossible to be versed on every hotel in every destination worldwide.

Another way to obtain information about hotels is through the LOCAL TOURIST BOARD/CONVENTION CENTER. They give generic information such as location, rates, number of rooms, and hotel classification. They cannot give you a personal opinion. They must remain impartial.

Many countries have an official grading system for hotels. These grading systems tend to rate hotels based on physical elements such as the size of the lobby or number of restaurants, rather than comfort. It is difficult to determine the condition or upkeep. A 2 star hotel in Europe may be adequate for a European, but Americans are used to their creature comforts and may find a standard 2 star hotel woefully inadequate.

If you are SEARCHING THE WEB, the sites I found to be useful are *hotels.com* or *expedia.com*. They have pictures of the hotel and a sample guest room, as well as basic information on amenities, restaurants and location. To look at a hotel description, you must input a travel date.

YOUR ABSOLUTE BEST SOURCE FOR HOTEL INFORMATION IS A TRAVEL AGENT SPECIALIZING IN YOUR DESTINATION. They have been there, have probably seen the hotel, and have excellent trade reference material. As mentioned before, you will have to pay a fee for this service from a travel agent.

Almost Ready to Book Your Hotel

You need to ask yourself these questions before you start poking around the web or calling a travel agent. These questions will point you in the best direction and cut down your surfing time or any hourly fee charged by the travel agent.

- Are your plans definite?
- Are you going to one specific place to do a specific activity?
- Are you willing to prepay your hotel reservation?
- Are you prepared to pay penalty fees if you change your plans?
- If you chose to use a travel agent, are you aware they charge service fees? Have you built this fee into your budget? (Estimate $50 per person, minimum, to be safe.)

Ways to Book Your Hotel Room

There are several ways to confirm a hotel room. You can:

- Call the hotel by telephone
- Call their central reservations office
- Book online with the hotel directly
- Book online with central reservations
- Book online through an online travel agency
- Book online through a hotel reservation service
- Buy a prepaid package
- Book with a travel agent.

Each source has a different way to secure, or hold, the hotel reservation.

Ways to Hold Your Reservation

Guaranteed Reservation: you give your credit card number to confirm the room. Nothing is charged unless you do not show up and neglect to call the hotel directly and cancel. Then your credit card will be charged a one night's rate plus tax, or whatever the policy is. Ask what is the specific cancellation policy for your hotel when confirming your reservation.

Pay a Deposit: either by check or credit card. Verify cancellation policy. As always, avoid paying any source by check for financial liability reasons. See Chapter 5 on budgets.

Fully Prepay the Room: by check or credit card. Usually this includes the tax and room only.

Prepay Room and Tax Through a Package: Most packages only include room and tax, but ask what you are actually paying and whom you are paying. Are you paying the hotel directly or are you paying through a middleman such as a tour operator or central reservations office? Know your source.

Prepay Room as Part of an All-Inclusive Program: same as above except "everything" is included: room, taxes, service charges, food, drinks, transfers, and limited sports. Verify what they mean by "everything." The term seems to take on different meanings with different sources.

Verify Cancellation Policies

Before you give your credit card to confirm your reservation, you must verify the cancellation and change policy of both the hotel you will be confirming and the booking source. Hotel cancellation policies vary from a generic 6:00 P.M. hold to a totally nonrefundable prepayment. If you are booking through an online hotel service, verify whether you are buying a totally nonrefundable non-changeable rate, or prepaying with only a $10 cancellation fee. If you book with a travel agent, you will probably be charged a cancellation fee for the time spent booking your trip.

A Note About Dates for Hotel Stays

When you look at the calendar, you are looking at the NIGHTS you will be staying. For instance, a November 21 to 24 hotel stay will be a 3-night stay, November 21, 22, 23, checking out 24. Rooms are sold in "24 hour blocks," where check-in is around 3:00 P.M. and check out is around 11:00 A.M. the next day. Specific times vary from hotel to hotel, location to location.

Early Arrivals: If your arrival is before 3:00 P.M., you should negotiate with the hotel for an early arrival time. If they have rooms available, they may allow you to check in early for no additional charge. But as is common in London, where travelers from the U.S. tend to arrive in the early morning around 7:00 A.M., you normally have to pay for the night before to get access to your room at 7:00 A.M. Sometimes the hotel will not charge you, depending on your repeat business and company affiliation or if they have many rooms available. If the hotel is sold out, you must confirm the room from the night before. Advise the hotel of your time of arrival so they will hold your room. You will have to pay the full night's rate for only a few hours' stay. Otherwise, you will be cranky, smelly and hanging out in the hotel bar waiting until they have a room cleaned, many hours later.

Late Check Outs: If you need your room past the 11:00 A.M. check out time, here again, you need to negotiate directly with the hotel. Trying to negotiate in advance will probably result in a charge for the extra time you need. Better yet, a few days before you arrive, check the availability for both the night you are staying and the second night, as if you were staying the full night. If they have all room types available for the second night, you can wait until you check in to negotiate for the late check out. You might get it for free. But if the second night is almost sold out, you will definitely be charged a fee for late check out or possibly refused the extra hours. In this case request the late check out as early as possible and ask for the "day rate" for this additional time.

Checking availability for your first night will give you an idea of how much leverage you have for the second night. If either night is sold out, you'll have little leverage.

Hotel Booking Check List

Now you are ready to take action. You have filled out the preplanning summary sheet at the end of part one and have your guidelines set. You now know:

- Who is going
- When are you going
- What you want to do on vacation
- Where you are going
- How much you can afford to spend per night.

From your hotel research you have determined:

- Which area you want to stay in—beach, downtown, etc.
- What hotel category you would like to stay in
- How many rooms and beds
- Type of hotel: regular hotel, suite-type, etc.
- Discounts you might be eligible for: AAA or AARP.

See Chapter 9.5, *Sources for Hotel Discounts.*

If you need help with the above go to the: *Hotel Check Off Sheet,* (Figure 9.1). The sheet is self-explanatory. Refer to Chapter 9, *Overview of Hotels,* for an explanation of the types and categories of hotels.

Hotel Reservation Sheet

See Figure 9.3 for the *Hotel Reservation Sheet.* It is included here to help you make a hotel reservation, whether you do it yourself or if you work with a travel agent. Read through the entire sheet before proceeding.

Which Booking Source Will You Use?

This is probably an easy question to answer. You are either Internet savvy or you're not. If you are familiar with the Internet, you could do it your usual way or you can go to the chapter, *Surf the Web for Hotels,* and follow the suggestions there. You could also use the telephone and call a hotel chain's toll-free central reservation office and book that way.

Whichever source you use, be sure to use the *Hotel Reservation Sheet* (make multiple copies first or download a copy from my website: *www.discounttravelwisdom.com*) to record all the information you gather. This is especially important if you book several hotels for the same date. You will then have to cancel the duplicate hotel reservations you won't be using, or your credit card will be charged a no-show fee.

Sample Hotel Research

Established Guidelines

Let's assume you have decided to travel to Orlando to visit Disney World, Universal Studios and several other touristy places. There will be 4 people—2 adults and 2 children, ages 6 and 8. You will have a rental car (compact size to be as economical as possible).

Your Basic Needs Include:

- One large room with 2 double beds or larger
- One bathroom
- Economical chain hotel
- Free parking.

Activities

- Visit theme parks
- Go swimming, at a park and hotel pool
- Shopping
- Location not important

The above guidelines are extremely basic and will be easy to find in Orlando. To help narrow down the search, let's add in a few features:

Possible Features

- Onsite theme park, economical property
- Suite hotel for added space
- Restaurant onsite, or nearby
- Kitchenette or refrigerator
- Pool

Estimated Budget

- 4 airline tickets, approx $300 each, total $1200
- Car rental, approx $300 for the week, intermediate-size car
- Theme park tickets, $950 for the 5-day Disney passes for the family
- Hotel up to $150 per night
- Food approx $150 day for family
- Misc. souvenirs, etc. $500

You would like to pay as much as possible by credit card and would prepay if necessary.

How to Find an Economical Hotel

First, you want to find a list of economical chain hotels. You can do this by checking with the tourist board, travel guidebooks such as Frommer's, your local travel agent, and online travel sites such as *Sidestep.com* or *Expedia.com*. You probably are looking for a 2- or 3-star property.

Then get a map of the area. (You could look up online at *mapquest.com*) In the Orlando example, locate on the map where the theme parks are, shopping areas, airport, and if there is a cluster of hotels anywhere. Note the names of the areas, i.e., Kissimmee, International Drive, Airport area.

Where will you spend most of your time? If it's at Universal Studios, you may want to find a hotel close by. In Orlando, however, it doesn't really matter where you stay if you have a car.

Next, what is your relative budget? How much can you afford?

With your travel guidelines in hand, start your research. Use the HOTEL RESERVATION SHEET to record your reservations. This sheet is a reminder to gather information you may need later, i.e., how you booked your hotel, cancellation policy, confirmation number, room category and size of bed.

Hotel Reservation Sheet

FIGURE 9.3

Hotel Name ______________________ City ______________________

Address: ______________________ Phone ______________________

In name of ______________ Age ___ And name ______________________ Age _____

Check In Date ______________ Day ______________ Est.Time of Arrival __________

Check Out Date ______________ Day ______________

Please note check in time is usually 3:00 P.M., check out time is usually 11:00 A.M. next day

❑ Nonsmoking ❑ Smoking ❑ Either one

Bedding type ❑ King ❑ Queen ❑ Double ❑ Twin ❑ Suite ❑ Other

Number of beds in room________ Location of room ______________________

Rate Per Night ______________ Number of Nights ______________

Rate Includes: Meals: ❑ None ❑ B ❑ L ❑ D ❑ All Inclusive

Hotel tax amount ______________ Other tax ______________ Service Charge ______________

Other ______________ Other ______________ Total Amount ______________

Use Credit Card # ______________________ Exp date ______________

❑ Guaranteed to credit card ❑ Deposit ______________ Amount ❑ Full prepayment ______________ Amount

Hotel's Cancellation Policy: ❑ 12PM ❑ 4PM ❑ 6PM ❑ 24 Hour ❑ 48 Hour ❑ 72 Hour ❑ 7 Days __________ Other

Booking Source:

Travel Agency ______________________ Agent ______________________

Website ______________________

Central Reservation Phone: ______________________ Agent ______________________

Telephone Number ______________________ Agent ______________________

Confirmation Number: ______________________ Date ______________________

Notes:

Cancellation Number ______________________ Date ______________________

Cancellation Charge ______________________ **Service Fee** ______________________

CHAPTER 9.4
Surf the Web for Hotels

If you have already read Chapter 8.3, *Surf the Web for Airfares,* this is basically the same, but with the focus on hotels. If you have jumped right to this hotel chapter, you should first go to the *Surf the Web for Airfares* chapter to get a better understanding of the process, especially the *Sidestep.com* plug-in browser.

It seems that every time I do research on the web, I find dramatic changes in the travel websites. They are continuously updating and improving the functioning of the sites. First, they worked on enhancing the airline websites. They got them in pretty good working order, too. Now the focus is on the hotel search websites. This is good, but you will see changes periodically until the bugs are worked out. No one hotel website has all the bargains. You still have to do multiple comparison searches to find the best rates. Eventually, it will balance out and leave the lackluster websites on the accounting room floor.

Currently, the choices offered below are the best hotel search sites that I've found. As other hotel search sites come online, this choice may change. Visit my website *discounttravelwisdom.com* for the latest information.

Where to Surf First

Just in case you are in a fog, launch your Internet browser, i.e., Microsoft Internet Explorer, first.

I would approach my surfing in this order:

1. Load *Sidestep.com* plug-in browser
2. Go to *hotels.com* and search there
3. Compare *Sidestep.com* results and redo
4. Call your travel agent, who probably can find you a better rate.

1. ***Sidestep.com***: download this plug-in browser first. If you are searching the Internet for anything travel-related, it is in your best interest to download the *Sidestep.com* plug-in browser. Most of the time it will automatically update itself when you launch a search (if it doesn't, you can click on the Sidestep icon on your internet toolbar—it looks like a coin with a plane on it—then start your search on the other site). When you go into one of the leading hotel reservation websites, *Sidestep.com* will launch a comparison search. You may have to request a search by clicking on Sidestep's comparison button.

Sidestep.com checks the actual availability for a hotel room by going directly into the individual hotel chain websites and into other major hotel vendor websites. They have also negotiated special rates for rooms from various hotels. Sidestep does not maintain a database of rates and availability. When you are ready to book, click on the "select" button and Sidestep links you directly to the vendor. You book on the vendor's site, not Sidestep's. Carefully read your screen for the policies of the reservation.

2. Go to *hotels.com*. This is the newest and most advanced hotel website of Hotel Reservation Network. HRN negotiates their hotel rooms in bulk and offers them for sale through their own website. The policy of *HRN/hotels.com* is that ALL reservations booked through them must be fully prepaid, including taxes, on a credit card. The reservations carry a $10 cancellation fee plus any charges the hotel may levy, so READ THE CANCELLATION POLICY section carefully.

IMPORTANT NOTE: *hotels.com* sends you an email with your confirmation code/number. Be on the look-out for this because you are still liable for the booking charges whether or not you receive the email. Call customer service, 1-800-2-hotels if you don't receive the email confirmation.

ANOTHER GOOD POINT TO NOTE: Because *hotels.com* negotiates rooms for every night of the year, they are a great source for those hard-to-get holiday or convention dates. They may have rooms, but at an inflated price.

3. DOUBLECHECK: *Sidestep.com.* I found that during its parallel search, Sidestep only picks up hotels with a two or three star rating. If you want more choices, then double-check *Sidestep.com.* On the left side of your screen—the Sidestep side—click on the modify search button at the very bottom. This will bring up several windows of options where you can

refine or expand your search. When I modified my search, I found many more hotel options, including many specially negotiated rates for Sidestep customers. There is also a profile window to request discount rates from AAA or AARP.

In Sidestep, if you find the same hotel and rate as you found on HRN, click on the select button and link directly to the hotel vendor. See how the room is secured. Is it guaranteed to a credit card or does it have to be prepaid? Most importantly, is it refundable? Many hotel chains offer discounted rates that are nonrefundable or nonchangeable. If you don't want to prepay your hotel (as is necessary through *HRN/hotels.com*) and the Sidestep hotel only needs a credit card guarantee, book with the Sidestep link. Also note, if the hotel requires a nonrefundable prepayment through *Sidestep.com*, it probably works the same through *hotels.com*.

4. TRAVEL AGENT: The computer systems that most travel agents subscribe to contain thousands of hotels worldwide. They are a wonderful booking source if the agent knows how to use the complicated hotel formats. I have repeatedly found cheaper rates at the same hotels in my GDS as compared to those I have found on the web. And most of the time, they needed only a credit card guarantee. Only prepay a hotel if your plans are locked in stone.

An advantage to booking through a travel agent and their computer system is that most of the hotels booked receive an instant confirmation. You will have an immediate answer. The travel agent can fax or email you a written confirmation through their computer system.

The travel agent can also book your hotel as part of a package. Quite often you can get the same rate as on the web, but with added value, something extra thrown in. Packages are usually prepaid and have heavy cancellation penalties attached. Expect to pay a service fee when working with a travel agent.

At present, I recommend you start by downloading the *Sidestep.com* plug-in browser. See Chapter 8.3, *Surf the Web for Airfares*, for how to do this. Then go to the home site of Hotel Reservation Network (HRN): *hotels.com*. They have umpteen million links, so be sure you are working with the site that says *hotels.com*.

Both *Sidestep.com* and *hotels.com* check actual availability for a hotel room. HRN has negotiated special rates for rooms from all their hotels for every night of the year and maintains their own database for availability. *Sidestep.com* also negotiates special rates with hotel chains and checks the individual reservation systems for availability. Sidestep does not maintain a database of rates and availability. Sidestep links you directly to the vendor and you book on the vendor's site, not Sidestep's. You must read your screen carefully for the specifics of the reservation. Are you only guaranteeing to a credit card or are you charging the entire stay, including tax, to your credit card? IT IS IMPERATIVE THAT YOU NOTE THE HOTEL'S CANCELLATION POLICY. EVERY ONE IS DIFFERENT. Whatever website you are on, go to the policies section to see how they operate. You must read that website's booking rules or call customer service. Know how that particular travel website works.

AUTHOR'S NOTE

Once you get a feel for what's available for your dates, go back to the airfare search section and see if the airline flights are still available. Hopefully, you have only searched at this point. NEVER book a nonrefundable airline ticket or hotel room unless you are certain you can get the other part of your trip confirmed at a reasonable price.

Bidding for Hotel Rooms on the Web

Hopefully you have your guidelines set (Are you tired of hearing this?). You have used the Hotel Check Off Sheet to focus your needs and have a hotel confirmed (under credit card guarantee only) using the Hotel Reservation

Sheet. But you are still over budget. The next step is to look for further discounts. If you haven't already done so, read the chapters on hotel and airline discounts. Some discounts that might apply are AAA and AARP. Anyone can join AAA; you have to be over 50 to join AARP. Both of these organizations have negotiated deep discounts almost everywhere, subject to rate availability. If you are still over budget, you may want to consider bidding for a hotel room.

How Bidding Works for Hotels

I have used the *priceline.com* website for the sample hotel bidding below. Kudos to *priceline.com* for creating a fast, easy to use, and very detailed, website.

FIRST, determine the amount per night you can afford. Include the taxes and miscellaneous fees. Estimate 15% extra if in doubt. The tax amount is not part of the original bid, but it will be added to the final billed amount. Also note that *priceline.com* charges a $5.95 processing fee per room.

THEN, determine the star rating or category that fits the amount you can afford. For help, see the star/category rating detail at *priceline.com* or go to *hotels.com* or *expedia.com* for names, pictures and general star categories of hotels.

ESTABLISH a bid amount for the room only; do not include tax, etc. Depending on how far in advance you are booking, the bid could start at 60% of the rates you found during your research (i.e., 40% less.)

GO TO a bidding site, such as *priceline.com*. Read how they work. *priceline.com* offers only blind purchases. You give them your dates, price, category, hotel location and credit card they then tell you where you are staying. The deal is locked in, nonrefundable. They don't care if you like the choice or use the room. They've got your money!

Priceline.com will tell you immediately if your bid is ridiculous but they will accept it regardless. If they process your bid and then reject it, you have to wait 72 hours before requesting the same area, dates and category again with *priceline.com*. But you can change the star category, increase your bid and re-bid immediately.

Priceline.com will send you an email acknowledgement and then a follow-up with an answer to your bid.

Last-Minute Travel

This is an area that is still developing. Currently, the best site to visit for U.S. travel is *site59.com*, a distressed merchandise travel website. You can book 14 days in advance, up to 3 hours prior departure. You can book hotel only, a hotel and air package, or hotel and car package. Everything is prepaid, nonrefundable and unchangeable. If you are definitely going, this is a great website to browse for hotel deals. As always, when dealing with a website, read the rules.

For the latest information about surfing hotel websites
send an e-mail to
tips@discounttravelwisdom.com

Handicaps of Using the Web for Hotels

- You need to know how to use a computer and the Web to do comparison shopping.
- You can spend hours searching. If you have spent 5 hours searching the web to save $10, a night is it a valuable use of your time?
- The Web can't offer you alternatives like a human being can.
- A travel agent can suggest a hotel that would better fit your needs. They would know whether it is a good value.
- A travel agent will give you booking alternatives. Should you only guarantee the room or would you get better value by including the hotel in a prepaid package?
- Sometimes you need the assurance of a human being. Someone you can ask a question, and get an answer from.
- You are responsible for reading and understanding all the "fine print."
- If you run into a problem, you are unlikely to get any help from the website's customer service department.
- You are financially liable for any hotel booking made online, whether or not you understood the cancellation policies of both the website and hotel.
- You are still financially responsible for any hotel booking made online, even if you did not get a confirmation email or fax.

Tips for Surfing the Web for Hotels

- Load *sidestep.com* onto your browser for that parallel search.
- Have your travel guidelines ready.
- As with any travel search, use the information gathered as a starting point in your research.
- Pay by credit card, not a debit/ATM card, check or cash.
- Purchase your hotel within 60 days of travel to be eligible for credit card protection.
- Make sure you have received a "confirmation" either by email, fax or letter.
- Review the confirmation. Make sure all the information is correct, especially the dates.
- Double-check your rate about a week before the hotel's cancellation period kicks in. If the rate goes down, call the hotel and ask them to honor the lower rate. If you have prepaid your hotel, you may not be able to change the rate; but you may be able to get the hotel to throw in a perk like breakfast.
- If you are particular about the size of your bed, review booking information before purchase. You may not be able to change it at the hotel.
- If the hotel you want is sold out, check another source. Tour operators and some hotel brokers buy rooms in blocks and may have space when the hotel is sold out.
- For last minute trips, 14 days or less, visit *site59.com* for any deals to your destination.
- For hard to get dates, i.e., a big convention in town or over a holiday, try *hotels.com*.
- Have lots of time and patience to do your search.

CHAPTER 9.5

Sources for Hotel Discounts

Hotel Reservation Savvy

There are several different ways to confirm a hotel reservation. You will probably need to compare the rates among several sources before finally committing to one. Chapter 9, *Hotel Research*, has information on how to find a hotel, hotel ratings, and how to book your hotel.

The ways to confirm a hotel are:

- Call the hotel's central reservation toll-free number.
- Call, fax, or email the hotel directly.
- With your computer savvy travel agent.
- Check availability over the Internet.
  - With an online hotel reservation service like *hotels.com*
  - Through online travel agencies like *expedia.com*
  - Through hotel chain websites like *Marriott.com*
- Through any company that sells travel, i.e., credit card companies, department stores, etc.
- Bid for your room at *priceline.com*.

First, you are in an information-gathering mode. Check online through *hotels.com* for a list of available hotels. Then check the hotel chain's website or call their toll-free reservation center.

If you do not use the Internet then your search is going to be more difficult. You need to find a list of hotels to call. You can best do this by checking with travel guides or tourist boards. Choose the rating or category you prefer, i.e., deluxe, moderate, or economy. It is best to find a hotel chain that fits your preferences. Call that central reservation toll-free number, or call a travel agent who can check their computer for available hotels. You'll have to pay a service fee for their help, but it's worth saving yourself the time, and they'll probably find you a great deal.

Tips for Getting a Lower Rate

- When booking your reservation, ask if there is a cheaper rate offered. Quite often there is. The agent just does not bother to look, and offers you the first rate that appears on their screen, which could be the regular rack rate—a non-discounted rate. The agent may also be instructed to sell the higher rates first.
- Check each night of your stay for lower rates. If you are staying from Wednesday through Sunday night, you might qualify for a weekend rate for Thursday, Friday, Saturday, or Sunday nights. Sometimes, booking several different rates is beyond the ability of the agent's computer skills, or a website is intentionally not programmed to check for lower rates.
- Be flexible about your arrival date. One day earlier or later may make a big difference. Many properties, especially resorts, base your rate on you check-in date. If you arrive in Las Vegas on a Saturday, you may be charged the inflated Saturday rate for each night of your stay. Arriving on Thursday could possibly save you 50% or more.
- Check for any promotional rates. Sometimes, for the same rate, you may get something included, such as breakfast, champagne, or free use of the health club. Or you might even get one night free if you stay X number of nights.
- Periodically call back or check online to see if the availability has changed and a cheaper rate is offered. This is especially true for Las Vegas.
- A few days before arrival, again, check for lower rates. If you have prepaid, be aware that there may be a cancellation or change fee to consider.
- Advise your hotel if you are celebrating any special event such as a honeymoon. If they do not give you a cheaper rate, they may throw in a perk like an upgraded room or a fruit basket.

Type of Discounts

Airline Tour Packages: Many airlines have their own tour departments. These airlines contract rooms for every night of the year, so they have tremendous buying power. This is passed on to you as cheaper hotel rates. The hotels they recommend are sold in conjunction with their airline seats and are subject to extensive scrutiny. The airline's reputation is at stake, so a bad hotel will rarely be sold. Keep in mind that you get what you pay for. Also note, international hotels have different standards from those in the U.S. What might be an acceptable tourist-class hotel in the U.S., such as Motel 6, the equivalent tourist-class category in Europe might be a total dump to an American.

AAA Discounts: Some of the best discounts are with AAA (American Automobile Association). You need your membership number to book. Call your local AAA office, any travel agent, book online with *Sidestep.com* or a hotel's toll-free number. The AAA rates are subject to availability so they may not always be offered. For a $65 per-year investment, you can save on hotels, cars, restaurants, shows and air. Anyone can become a member. You do not need to own a car to join. Call your local AAA office to join or enroll online at *www.aaa.com.*

AARP: American Association of Retired Persons: This organization is the number one lobbyist group with the U.S. government because of its buying power. AARP can negotiate for deep discounts because of the immense volume it can generate. This is especially true for the travel industry. I have seen many discounted rates that were half the rack rate. Their rates are capacity controlled at many properties. Anyone over the age of 50 can join for a fee of $12.50 per year.

Call 1-800-424-3410 or join online at *www.aarp.com.*

Airline Frequent Flyer Programs: Programs vary, so check with your airline for award benefits. The hotel awards are being phased out at some airlines. The coupons offered with air ticket awards tend to be difficult to redeem. You can usually find a discount elsewhere.

Bid for a Hotel Room: See Chapter 9.4, *Surf the Web For Hotels,* for the best way to bid for a hotel room.

Convention Rates: Conventions think they have a captured audience, and usually inflate hotel rates. Hotels claim that they have to charge a higher amount to cover the extra staff needed to handle a large group checking in around the same time. This is very typical in a convention city such as Las Vegas where all the hotel rooms are controlled by the convention organizers. Rooms can be bought only through them and are normally prepaid and nonrefundable. But sometimes you can find a discount from an airline tour desk if you tell them you are not going to the convention. As always, check availability closer to arrival for any cheaper rates opening up.

Also note, to get a room in a "sold out" city, you might try *hotels.com*. They may buy rooms in bulk for sold-out days and offer them for sale at a higher than normal rate. If you can't find a room, *hotels.com* (1-800-2-hotels) is a great source.

Corporate Rates/Consortiums: These are negotiated rates based on volume promised. Consortiums are groups of travel agents pooling their bookings through one organization for greater discounts. Large corporations, such as IBM, can negotiate for special corporate discounts because the can promise huge volume.

Government or Military Rates: These are the deepest discounts I have seen. You must present your government employee identification card at check-in. Verify the booking requirements. Some hotels may want you to call them directly for this discount.

Hotel Frequent Stay Programs: Similar to the airline programs, it is wise to enroll in several hotel frequent stay programs and concentrate your stays at one or two of them. Join a program like Marriott who has several sister chains: Courtyard, Renaissance, Residence Inn, etc., or Starwood Hotels, which includes the various Sheraton products, Westin and W hotels. Sometimes you can double up on miles—receive hotel and airline miles. Use the free night awards to pay for expensive stays.

Hotel Brokers/Consolidators: It is very risky to use them. You can usually get a better deal somewhere else without all the restrictions. Brokers buy rooms in bulk and must pay for the rooms whether or not they sell them. Be sure to get all the rules BEFORE giving your credit card. Most of the time you must prepay every night of your stay. Usually you CANNOT change it or get a refund. If they do allow changes or cancellations you may have to pay a hefty fee. When booking, get the rate, type of bedding, location of room, and whether anything is included in the rate, such as taxes, service, meals, etc. Ask whether there will be any surcharges levied by the hotel when you check in. If the only way you can confirm a hotel in a sold-out city is through a broker, then make sure you get a written confirmation or voucher. Immediately call the hotel directly and verify that they have the reservation and whether they accept the broker's hotel voucher as payment. If you do this right away, you can prevent not having a room in a sold-out city when you get there.

Internet: Most hotel chains have an online booking site. Just like the airlines, some chains offer a discount or a bonus if you book online. Verify policies for prepayment, guarantee, and cancellations. Many chains offer nonrefundable prepaid rates.

Membership or Travel Clubs: These are organizations that offer various discounts including travel products like airline, hotel, and car rental discounts. They require you to purchase a year-long membership in order to utilize these discounts. Sometimes they require you to purchase the travel product in full from them only. They tend to not allow you to change your mind once you have paid for the product. Again, buyer beware. Make sure you get in writing the terms of what you are buying. Also check with the Better Business Bureau for any complaints.

Weekend Rates: These rates can be half of the rack rates. The hotels tend to offer only a certain number of rooms at this discounted rate. The timing of your call makes all the difference. Call far in advance to get a room from the initial block. Call again within 7 days of arrival. This is when hotels reassess their room bookings (yield management) and may add more of the discounted rates to spark business. For hotels in major cities where business travel is only Sunday through Thursday, they may offer weekend rates Thursday, Friday, and/or Saturday nights, again, capacity controlled. Verify whether the rate includes breakfast. Resort areas tend to not offer weekend rates.

Tips for Finding Hard-to-Get Rooms

- Check with *hotels.com*, 1-800-2-hotels, for any blocked space. They buy or negotiate rooms for every night of the year, including hard-to-find convention dates and holidays.
- If buying an airline ticket, check with your airline's tour desk. They, too, buy blocks of rooms throughout the year. And, you can possibly get a discount on the airfare!
- Have your travel agent call the hotel to find out whether the hotel is still holding unsold rooms for any wholesalers/tour operators. They usually release unsold rooms 4–6 weeks prior arrival., The travel agent can also call the wholesaler and purchase the room from them.
- See a travel agent or look online for packages. As above, hopefully any availability you see means the vendor is holding the room.

Part Five: Choosing Car Rentals

Chapter 10	Choosing Car Rentals	155
Chapter 10.1	Car Rental Discounts	166

CHAPTER 10

Choosing Car Rentals

This is another area of mass confusion. The way the car companies calculate their rates requires a higher math degree and a stopwatch. Rates vary depending on the day and time of pick up, how long you keep the car, the exact hour you return it, how many miles you drive, the size of the car, and if you take the shuttle bus from the airline terminal. The biggest mystery is the number of extra fees that appear on your rental contract. Should you or should you not buy that collision damage waiver for a gazillion extra dollars a day? The agent is personally very concerned that you'll have to shell out the price of the car if you get into an accident and insists you should buy it. (They actually make a nice commission if they get you to buy it. Hence the heavy sales pitch and pressure tactics.)

You Must Have a Credit Card to Rent a Car

In order to rent a car you must have a credit card. This credit card must have available enough credit to pay for your complete car rental, including insurance, gas, taxes, etc., and then some. When you pick up your car, the car rental company holds against your credit card either the estimated cost of your car rental OR the entire value of the car! They do a credit check to see whether you're a deadbeat and a DMV check to see if there are any outstanding charges against your driver's license.

How Big a Car Should You Rent?

This depends on the number of people who will ride in the car, how much luggage you have, how much driving you will be doing, what outdoor activities you plan on doing, and how long you will need the car. Rule of thumb: get a bigger one than you think you will need. There usually is a small difference in price to upgrade to a larger car, and it may make a huge difference in the quality and comfort of your trip.

Which Car Company Should You Rent From? Rent from the one with the best rate. They all pretty much provide the same service, or lack of service. If you have a frequent renter ID number, you probably would rent from that company or at least check their rates first.

Corporate Discount Contract: If your employer has a corporate contract with discount rates, you may want to use that company for your vacation too. Even though some corporate contracts allow only the special benefits such as insurance coverage for legitimate business rentals, you can still take advantage of the discounted rate. Just make sure the credit card you charge it to has collision coverage. Also check you own car insurance policy.

Car Rental Rates

The rate that is quoted in most booking sources is just the basic rate, daily, weekend, or weekly. Then the additional charges kick in. They can double the amount you pay, possibly adding an additional 40 percent or more, and do major damage to your budget. Here is a partial list of rates, extra charges, taxes and fees. Every day someone somewhere comes up with another charge to soak the visitor.

Basic Rates

Unlimited Mileage Rate: This is the most common rate offered in high-demand locations. These also vary, like the price of an airline seat. The rate depends on the availability of cars, how far in advance you book, and whether you have any type of discount.

- **Daily Unlimited Mileage Rate:** Usually applies to cars picked up (rented) on a week day, Monday through Friday. The extra day rate is usually the same amount.
- **Weekend Unlimited Mileage Rate:** Pick up the car anytime between Thursday and Saturday. Varies by location. Sometimes the rate has a 2- or 3-day minimum rental, or you must keep the car over a Saturday night. High-demand city locations such as New York City actually charge more for weekend rentals. The rate could be lower if you rent on a Thursday than if you rent on a Saturday. I've often rented on a Thursday and parked the car for a day to get a cheaper rate! (But then I have to deal with the NYC alternate-side parking situation!)
- **Weekly Rates:** This refers to seven 24-hour periods. The 8th day, etc., is billed at the extra day rate, which is rarely one-seventh of the weekly rate, and more like 50% of the weekly rate. So if you are renting for 10 days, you could be paying one and one half times more than the base rate. It would actually be cheaper to rent for 2 weeks (or a minimum of 12 days) instead of 10 days. The weekly rate is allowed for rentals of 5 days to 7 days.

Time and Mileage Rates: The rate per day allows a certain number of miles driven included in the rate, i.e., $20.95/day, 250 miles free. When you exceed the miles allowed you pay a hefty per-mile fee, say 25¢ per mile. If you are not planning to drive much, this shouldn't matter, but if you are, hunt around for a car company that offers an unlimited mileage rate. In areas of minimal demand, you may have to scout around for a reasonable unlimited mileage rate.

Those Extra Charges

This is a truly bottomless pit of invention. I've been charged for spark plugs, battery charging, parking ticket fee donations, convention centers and, of course, that famous shuttle bus. Every city has different fees added that are mandatory. This information may not appear on the rental contract when you pick up the car and totally surprise you when you get the final bill. This could add another 40 % or more to the cost of your basic rate.

When you make your reservation, ask the agent for the extra charges that will be added to your bill. Internet bookings may or may not provide this information. Here is a run down of some of the added taxes and fees:

- State taxes
- Local/city taxes
- Federal taxes
- 10% for airport access (that bus you took)
- $2.05 per day Florida surcharge/tire fee
- 40¢ per day vehicle license recovery fee
- 3¢ per day recycling fee recovery
- 7.5% frequent flyer excise tax fee to get your frequent flyer points (and you thought they came free!)
- $10 per rental to pay for a new convention center in Boston
- 30¢ parking fine recovery fee
- 8.8% for the vehicle's registration
- Extra driver, over 25 years old, can add $4 to 25 per day
- Baby car seats, an extra $3 to 10 per day
- Under-age surcharge, drivers 21 to 25 years old can be charged up to ***$100*** per day more if the rental is allowed. If on business, using a corporate credit card and utilizing the corporate rate, this fee may be waived.
- Fuel purchase option. If purchased, bring car back with an empty fuel tank. No refund for gas left in tank.
- Refuel that tank or pay dearly for the empty portion. The car companies have an inflated idea of the price of gas, $3.50 to $6.00 per gallon. So fill up that tank.
- One-way rentals: If you rent in one city and return to another, the base rate will be high and include a drop off fee of possibly hundreds of dollars. You can save money if you rent from National Rent a Car. They have slightly higher daily unlimited mileage rates that incorporate the one-way fee into a higher base rate.

What Is the Collision Damage Waiver?

The collision damage waiver, or loss damage waiver, as it is sometimes called, is "insurance" coverage for the RENTAL CAR YOU ARE DRIVING

ONLY. This is the coverage offered by many credit card companies and auto insurance companies on your own car. It does NOT cover the damage to the other car, any property damage, or any personal injury. You would need liability insurance to cover those.

Should You Buy Collision Damage Coverage?

Probably not. You probably have coverage from another source such as your own car insurance, business car insurance or credit card benefits. The coverage offered by the car rental company at $20 or so per day is not necessary if you have other coverage. It's just a way for the car rental company to make more money. The rental agent also may get a hefty commission from this.

Call your various insurance and credit card companies to see what coverage you already have.

How Does This Differ from Liability Insurance?

The collision damage waiver only covers the car you have rented and are driving. It does not cover damage to the other car, property or people. For this you need some kind of liability insurance. This is offered separately by the rental company and usually requires you to initial that you are declining this coverage. It is often called SLI—Supplemental Liability Insurance. This covers claims made for damage to the other car, for people injured or killed, or for property damage. The cost is around $15 per day and may give only a small amount of medical or death benefits coverage. Check the individual car rental companies for their coverage. For example, Hertz in Orlando charges $10.99 per day and covers up to $1 million dollars in total benefits.

Check with your insurance broker for a policy that may cover you all year if you travel a lot.

Should You Buy Supplemental Liability Insurance?

This is totally up to you. It depends on your peace of mind. If you get into an accident and someone is killed, can you financially survive a million-dollar lawsuit? $10.99 per day seems cheap in comparison.

Should You Buy PAI— Personal Accident Insurance?

Again, this is up to you. See if you have coverage on your car or homeowners policies. PAI covers your personal effects while they are in the car or in your hotel room for the length of the rental contract.

Should You Buy PEC— Personal Effects Insurance?

Your homeowners' or renters' insurance policy may already cover you. If you choose to buy this additional insurance, ask what it covers. It may not cover the real valuable stuff such as your laptop computer, cash or jewelry. And the $600 coverage you get may not be worth the paperwork.

Back to that Collision Damage Waiver

If you already own a car, your car insurance usually kicks in first; this is called your primary insurance. Your credit card coverage, if it applies, will be considered secondary insurance. If you do not own a car with car insurance, then your credit card coverage is considered primary insurance. It will be the insurance you will use if you have a car accident.

RE: YOUR CAR INSURANCE POLICY: Call your broker or insurance company and ask about any rental car coverage. Find out:

- If it covers damage to the car you rent, the other car, property or people.
- Is there a deductible? How much?
- Does it cover for the rental company's "loss of use" charge—revenue lost while the car is being repaired? This is added to the claim if the car rental company can get away with it!
- Which car types are covered?

Credit Card Coverage

Please, please call your credit card companies and ask, and get in writing, their policy about car rental insurance coverage. Give them your credit card number, as not all types of cards issued by the same credit card company have car rental insurance coverage included. The "regular" cards usually do not. Gold, platinum or other specialty cards probably do.

FIND OUT:

- Which car types are covered? Usually specialty cars, sports cars, pick up trucks, vans or even the all-popular SUV may NOT be covered. Vehicles that carry over 15 people or only cargo are NOT usually covered.
- Whether the length of rental matters. Generally less than 30 days is covered.
- If the collision coverage is for the entire cost of the car.
- Is there a deductible? How much?
- Does it cover the rental car company's "loss of use" charge? (Revenue lost while car is being repaired) If not, find another credit card that does.
- Does it cover for international rentals? This varies.
- You are probably covered for renting anywhere in the United States.
- Verify trans-border coverage. You may not be covered if you go into Mexico. You will have to buy special coverage for this. This also varies among the car rental companies, so shop around.
- Avoid upgrading to a larger car simply because it is offered to you at the same price as the smaller one. The larger one, say an SUV, may not be covered by the credit card collision benefit. Call your credit card company from the rental counter and verify whether you have coverage.

The AMERICAN EXPRESS CARD (see your statement for phone number) has many different types of credit cards and benefit plans. A gold card may not necessarily include coverage. It depends on the card agreement. SO CALL AMEX AND GIVE YOUR ACCOUNT NUMBER AND SEE IF YOU ARE COVERED. Don't wait till you have an accident and find out when it's too late that you are not covered. Also the type of car, length of rental, and international destinations vary by card number. SO CALL.

When I last spoke with my favorite credit card company, DINERS CLUB (1-800-2-DINERS), all their card types cover most everything. Their insurance is considered primary insurance, covers all car types under 15 passengers, valid in all 50 states, Canada, Mexico, worldwide, and is valid for trans-border crossings. The length of rental coverage varies—30 days for a personal card, 45 days for a corporate card.

The DISCOVER CARD (1-800-347-2683) coverage is valid for gold and platinum cards only, NOT the regular card. Their insurance is considered secondary insurance, so your own car policy kicks in first. You are covered for rentals in the United States and Canada, but not Mexico. If you have another card with car rental coverage, you might do better by using them instead. Discover's benefits are not as good as some of the other card companies.

When Is Your Credit Card Benefit Valid?

The benefits kick in when you give your credit card and driver's license to the rental agent at the time of pick up. The credit card, and all insurances you want coverage from, must be on the original rental contract agreement. Otherwise it is not valid. Once you sign the rental contract you are covered.

- You cannot change the credit card or add insurance after you have an accident and expect coverage. It does not work that way.
- You must also ***decline*** the collision damage waiver offered by the car rental company. That coverage would apply if you did buy it.
- Obviously if you pay with cash, you have no coverage unless you buy it. (Not recommended)

Be Wary of Scams

People on vacation tend to be targets for unscrupulous car rental agents. They take advantage of your inexperience with travel details. They may out and out lie to you. You must know what your rights are and stand firm when they pressure you to buy the expensive collision/loss damage waiver. You could possibly get pressure from all the car companies, especially in heavy tourist areas like Florida or Arizona cities.

When you are at the rental counter, the agent may ask you the name of your insurance company. Call your credit card company and ask. Have ready the name of the company your credit card uses. I had a difficult time with Alamo rent a car in Florida. The agent was insistent that I give the name of the insurance company and would not accept the name "American Express Card insurance." The Alamo agent was trying to intimidate me into buying the daily collision waiver, which I did not need. (The agent

AUTHOR'S NOTE

Renter's Courtesy

When you have a problem with your rented car, such as a broken windshield wiper, out of washer fluid, oil light or a warning light comes on, be sure to advise the check-in agent or the roving person with the hand-held gadget, that you had a problem. This will alert the service agent to check over the car and fix the problem. I don't know how many cars I have rented that have had annoying little inconveniences or big ones like NO GAS IN THE TANK. A little common courtesy goes a long way for the next renter.

actually walked away to avoid dealing with me. I did finally rent the car without the added collision insurance.)

I faced another pressure tactic from Enterprise in Phoenix, AZ, recently. The counter agent repeatedly stated that if I declined the collision damage waiver I would be liable for the daily rate of $33.95/day for every day the car was in the shop for repairs if I had an accident. He went so far as to circle the amount on the contract, and pointed to it several times even after I declined to buy the unneeded insurance. Verify if your credit card company covers this "loss of use" clause.

Also, credit card car insurance coverage is valid for the United States and Canada. Any claim that says it is not valid in that city or state is a scam. (The car rental company may have a restriction on what states you can drive in. They may use a satellite-tracking device to keep an eye on you.)

It might be a good idea to take the credit card coverage information with you on your trip, or call your company from the rental counter to verify coverage.

A Story About Gasoline

I once rented a car from National Rent a Car in New York City. The gas tank was on empty. When I mentioned this to the rental agent he said, no problem, "I will just indicate on your rental contract that the tank was empty. Bring it back empty and you won't be charged for gas." I stupidly accepted this, figuring I could get gas at the station around the corner from my house in Queens. Wrong. I went 10 blocks and the "out of gas" light went on. Instead of taking the car back to the location and exchanging it, or insisting that they fill the tank, I elected to go on home. I was fortunate that there was no traffic on the bridge to Queens or I never would have made it home, 4 miles away. The moral of this story: make sure you have at least a half a tank of gas and note the amount on your rental contract. This is the amount of gas you must put in the car before returning it. Otherwise, the car rental company will charge you to fill the tank, for a normally grossly inflated amount, such as $4.75 a gallon! If you purchase the fuel purchase option, you return the tank empty. If in doubt, ASK THE RENTAL AGENT WHERE THE LEVEL THE GAS TANK MUST BE IN ORDER TO NOT BE CHARGED FOR GAS.

The Fuel Purchase Option: Whether or not you buy it depends on your gas buying preferences. The rate charged for the fuel purchase option is the local going rate, not the inflated rate the car rental companies charge for refueling. You must decide to buy it when you pick up the car, and it must be indicated on the rental contract to be valid. You cannot decide after you have used the gas that you want the promo. If you take this option, you bring the car back with an empty tank. You do not get any refund for gas left in the car. I like this option because I'm always in a hurry to return the car and hate having to hunt around for a gas station to refuel. I try to leave as little as possible in the tank. I also like that part of the gasoline expense is charged on the rental contract. I hate having to get receipts and itemize gas expenses.

Money-Saving Tips

- Do your homework in advance to avoid surprises at the rental counter.
- Always ask at the counter if there is a cheaper rate available. If they have lots of cars on the lot, they may be willing to negotiate. Also mention whether you have any discounts such as AAA, AARP, frequently flyer, or corporate discounts.
- If you give your frequent flyer number to get miles, keep in mind that you could be charged the 7.5% tax recovery surcharge on the

entire bill. To get 500 miles, you could be billed an additional $25. This is no longer a good frequent flyer benefit, but a phony "perk."

- It may be cheaper to keep the car for an extra day to get the weekly rate. A weekly rate is billed for 5 to 7 days.
- By renting a day earlier or later, you might get a weekend rate. Compare dates.
- Some discounted rates require you to keep the car over a Saturday night. If you rent a car from Sunday to Saturday, you could possibly end up paying the higher daily rate.
- Rates are calculated on a 24-hour period. After 24 hours, the extra hour rate kicks in. Two extra hours could end up being another day's rental rate. BEST TO WATCH THE CLOCK. Usually an hour grace period is allowed. If you keep the car for an additional 61 minutes. you will be charged an extra hour rate. If they do not give you the hour grace, ask for a supervisor. Or pay the bill and write a letter to the corporate office's customer service department.

For example: the weekend daily rate in Boston could be $38.99 per day for an intermediate size car. (Friday to 11 A.M. on Monday) If you keep the car for an extra 61 minutes, until 12:01 P.M., you will be charged the extra-hour rate of $32 per hour for the extra minute. (One hour grace period plus one minute.) If you return the car after 1:01 P.M., you will be charged a full day's rate. But the weekend rate of $38.99 no longer applies. If you don't return the car by 11:00 A.M. on Monday, the regular weekday rate applies. In this case, ***$63.99 per day!*** You are being penalized for being an hour late.

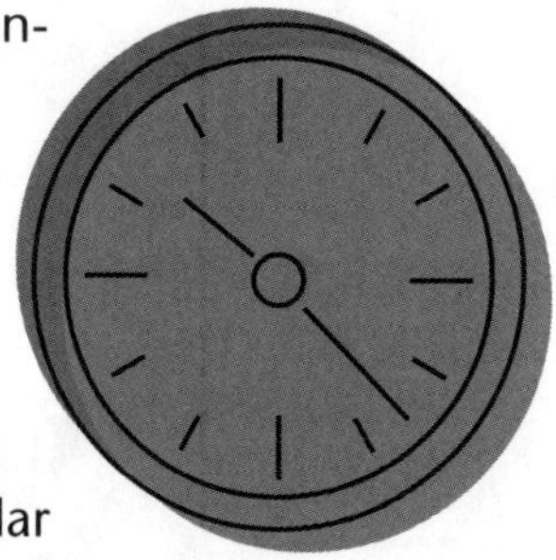

- Return the car with the correct amount of gas. If it was full when you picked up the car, return it full or be subject to a whopping fee of $5 or more per GALLON.
- Use a credit card that has the collision damage waiver coverage for car rentals. This could save you from purchasing coverage at $20 per day. Not all credit cards have it, so call and ask, and upgrade your card to a gold card if necessary, to get coverage.

Trip Cancellation Insurance: Should You Buy It?

Most of the time, you do not need to buy additional coverage. Your homeowners, car insurance, medical plan or credit cards have coverage. Call them prior to travel to see what coverage you have. Any pressure by someone selling you insurance (car companies are notorious) is because the counter agent can personally make extra commission for something you do not need.

For the latest information about surfing car websites send an e-mail to *tips@discounttravelwisdom.com*

CHAPTER 10.1
Car Rental Discounts

The car rental companies have learned new tricks from the airlines—offer different rates depending on your source of booking and when you make your reservation.

Tips

- Absolutely make a reservation in advance. Many discounted rates must be booked 24 hours in advance. The rates quoted to you at the car rental counter are usually grossly inflated.
- Car sizes are as follows, smallest to largest: economy, compact, mid-size/intermediate, standard-2 door, full size-4 door, premium, and luxury.
- Select the car category that you would be most comfortable driving, i.e., compact vs. intermediate size.
- For more trunk space and comfort, chose a size larger than you think you need, especially if you have 3 or more passengers.
- Most cars have 4 doors, but you can get stuck with a 2-door if you don't specify you want a 4-door when booking. If, when picking up your car, the car rental company is low on cars, they may try to "upgrade" you to the next size car AND charge you more. If you have a guaranteed rate and car size, they should upgrade you for free. It's not your fault that they ran out of your car size.

Compare Rates Among Booking Sources

Also see the following section: tips for surfing the web.

- Call the car rental company's central reservation center and ask for the lowest rate. Remember, you are dealing with a human being making minimum wage, so ask if there are any other discounts you may be eligible for. Keep encouraging them to search further.

- If you are a member of an airline frequent flyer program, advise the agent. Most airlines have a standard discount with the major car rental companies. You may only be able to use the discount from the airline you are flying in on.
- Have your travel agent check their computer for the best rate.
- Go online and see if there are any promotions offered.
- Call or visit the local rental office for any "walk up" specials. (FYI—Sometimes if you call one of the locations of a major car rental company, you may be automatically transferred into their nation wide central reservation center.)
- Repeat all of the above steps again 2–3 weeks prior to the pick up date.

Tips for Surfing the Web for Cars

Conduct you Internet surfing as you would for an airline ticket. Have your car guidelines ready:

1. Load the *Sidestep.com* plug-in to your browser.
2. Search with *expedia.com* or *travelocity.com* (this will trigger Sidestep to open. Request a comparison search with *Sidestep.com.*
3. Check with your travel agent for any corporate or travel agent consortium discounts.

This should save you time and narrow down your choices. Obviously, you want to book with the least expensive and most reliable car company. Renting from "Fly By Nite Drive By Day" car company to save $10 may cost you more in the long run if the car breaks down.

Sources for Car Discounts

AAA Rates: Automobile Association of America—requires membership, call 1-800-564-6222. Or enroll via the web at *aaa.com.* This is the best program for non-corporate clients. You don't need to own a car to become a member.

Airline Frequent Flyer Programs: Each airline has negotiated rates with specific car companies. Call your airline frequent flyer desk for the negotiated car rental discount number. You can also ask the agent at the car company to look up the number for you.

Airline Tour Packages and Tour Operator Packages: Tour operators negotiate special rates for prepaid car rentals. Sometimes, but not always, their rates can be cheaper that what you get on your own. This applies especially over peak holiday periods. Usually you must prepay the basic rental cost, and then it is nonrefundable. Ask what extras you must pay for at the counter. Also see *site59.com* for last-minute air and car packages.

Corporate Rates: Most large corporations negotiate deeply discounted rates for their employees. Obtain the corporate discount ID numbers from the company's travel coordinator. Please note: If booking via a travel agent, there may be a service fee involved. The car companies no longer pay commission to travel agents for these often time-consuming bookings.

Priceline.com has a name-your-own-price car rental program with 5 major car rental companies: Alamo, Avis, Budget, Hertz, and National. Their website says you can save 20% or more. Remember, these are prepaid *nonchangeable* and *nonrefundable* rates. Do your homework first and find out the going rate for your dates. Make your initial bid offer at least 10–14 days prior to pick-up dates. You can make a bid for the same dates only once a week. If your bid is rejected, you have to wait a week to try again. Or you could bid at a different site.

Promos and Coupons are everywhere:

- Car sales departments give coupons to travel agents and corporate travel departments.
- In car and travel magazines.
- Ask the rental agent for a discount.

For international cars, websites like *autoeurope.com* or *kemwell.com* run sales periodically throughout the year. Look for them.

Weekend/Holiday Rates: Many locations offer weekend or holiday rates, so ask. I also discovered a very expensive rate in Florida over Christmas ($400 per week, nothing included) that was booked several months in advance, actually went down by $200 a few weeks prior to pick up date. BUT this will only happen if the car rental location has a surplus of cars. Cars tend to sell out far in advance over Christmas. If you want a car over Christmas in Florida, it is best to confirm as far in advance as possible, and double check the rate a few weeks prior to arrival. Please note, many car rental companies only guarantee the rate quoted for 3 months from the time you made the reservation. The rate can go up if you book more than 3 months in advance. This becomes a juggling act.

International Car Discounts

Although various big car companies offer "discounted" fully prepaid car programs, I have found these rates are not competitive. They tend to offer prepaid rates that do not include taxes and fees. They many not advise you these are extra and payable when you pick up the car. These extra fees and taxes can add as much as 40% to your basic rental cost. Be sure to ask exactly what is being prepaid, and what charges are paid locally (at the rental counter). Do you pay a deposit, or is full prepayment required? Can you change the reservation once you have prepaid? Is it a NONREFUNDABLE PREPAYMENT? You will need to know what is included for a proper comparison. Some companies omit a tax or two to make their rates look competitive when they are not. Have your travel agent call the following companies for the best inclusive rates:

Autoeurope, (1-800-223-5555), *autoeurope.com*—my favorite. They are extremely easy to work with and have the best rates. They have expanded from Europe into Australia and South Africa. Most of the time they include taxes and other miscellaneous charges. Be sure to ask exactly what is being prepaid, and what charges are paid locally (at rental counter). Do you pay a deposit, or is a full prepayment required? Does it include the airport taxes and fees? Most of the rates with AutoEurope are fully refundable and cancelable at almost any time. AutoEurope also is an AIR consolidator.

Kemwell, (1-877-820-0668), *kemwel.com*—another car consolidator, owned by Autoeurope. Both companies offer a price match guarantee. If you get a quote elsewhere for the same product, they will match it and give you $10.

Hertz—I find their rates always seem to have something missing and require a prepayment that usually is NONREFUNDABLE (which I don't consider competitive). Best to use AutoEurope.

Last-Minutes Specials

Hertz.com: visit the LAST-MINUTE SPECIALS section for discounts in the U.S. Updated on a regular basis.

Priceline.com: can still be a good deal at the last minute, again, nonrefundable, non-changeable. Do your research so you know the going rates and have a basis for your bid.

Site59.com: if you are also buying an airline ticket, you can get a discounted package with air and car, no hotel necessary, within 14 days of travel. Nonrefundable, nonchangeable.

Part Six: Should You Buy a Package?

Chapter 11 Packages, Tours, and All-Inclusives 173

CHAPTER 11

Packages, Tours, and All-Inclusives

The general public has been duped into thinking that a prepaid package saves money. Sometimes it does, especially if the package originates from a high-volume reputable wholesaler such as Gogo Tours. But the savings that was initially built into a package vanishes if the availability is reduced by high demand. Although significant discounts may vanish, you do get the convenience of locking in your travel plans by prepaying. Quite often buying a package over the holidays is the only way to get a room and air space confirmed. And the travel agent gets a commission from the wholesaler. Because they get a guaranteed payment, the travel agent may not charge you a service fee if you buy a prepaid package.

When you buy a prepaid package, you must be absolutely sure that you are going. Any changes or cancellations incur heavy penalties or may be totally nonrefundable or non-changeable.

What Are Packages, Tours, and All-Inclusives?

A Package is made up of features that are bundled together and sold for one price. The basic features of a package may include airfare, hotel, transfers, and some taxes, and sold one package at a time.

A Tour is also a prepaid package but sold to a group of unrelated people. It would require a minimum number of people for the tour to happen. A tour usually includes added features such as sightseeing or specialty meals. If you don't participate in any portion of the tour, you do not get a refund. Often a "tour escort" is provided to coordinate details during your trip.

An All-Inclusive is a tour package that supposedly includes everything—airfare, transfers, lodging, taxes, service charge, all meals and possibly snacks, beverages and alcohol, non-motorized sports and entertainment. How "all-inclusive" a property is depends on revenues and how management translates the term.

Some Notes About Packages

Features are items such as airfare, hotel, transfers, meals, tours, sightseeing, and taxes that are included in the package or tour.

Wholesalers are the folks who put together the features to sell to you via the travel agent. Most of the time the wholesaler does not sell directly to the general public. A few do, to bypass paying commission to the travel agent. This does not mean that the package price is lower. It means the wholesaler makes more money and you probably get less service for the same price.

Travel Agents play a very important role. They are your policemen. They know which wholesaler will deliver the product purchased, and which wholesaler is financially stable. The travel agent will match you to the package that fits your needs. They also will go to bat for you if there is a problem.

The Brochure is a composite of what the wholesaler wants to sell you. Hopefully it will describe the included features, dates they want to sell you, prices, pictures, and a page of legalese to cover their butts.

Bulk Airfare: This is where you get your savings when booking a package. If available, the airfare that is sold with a package is called a "bulk fare." This "bulk fare" is a negotiated discounted airfare that is capacity controlled and can be sold only in conjunction with another feature such as a hotel, transfers/car rental or tour feature. You could save $100 to $200 on tickets to the Caribbean if the capacity controlled inventory is available. If not, you are probably buying a nonrefundable airfare through a third party, the wholesaler, not the travel agent you are speaking to. Here again it's a matter of convenience, and whether or not you want to pay in advance.

Why Buy a Package or Tour?

So you can have the major portion of your trip prepaid before you leave. Prepaying helps you to stay within your budget. Also, sometimes a package or tour comes with added benefits such as a room upgrade, a meal, or bottle of champagne.

Certain destinations, such as the Caribbean, are usually a better value if you prepay your vacation. The bigger wholesalers get better rates and can pass them on to you at a slight savings. Also, most hotels in resort areas require full prepayment far in advance. Sometimes it is easier to get your money back from a wholesaler who has less stringent cancellation policies with the hotels than if you deal with the hotel directly. See change and cancellation policy section below.

How to Buy a Package or Tour

See a travel agent, see the chapter, *How to Find a Reliable Travel Agent*. Or you can book online with a reputable travel search engine such as *site59.com*, a last-minute booking site. The travel agent will guide you along the correct path by qualifying you: they will try to determine what it is you really want and then match you to a prepaid package. (Follow the instructions in Part 1, *Preplanning*, if you want to buy online). When buying from a travel agent, booking a package is extremely time-consuming, so be prepared to pay a service fee for their time and expertise.

If You Decide to Buy a Package from a Travel Agent

One of the best reasons for using a leisure travel agent is their knowledge about the various packages and all-inclusive properties and what you can expect from your vacation. If you run into a problem, they will go to bat for you. For example, if you paid for a deluxe ocean-front room but got one in the back by the dumpster, the travel agent can call and get you the room you paid for. If you buy online, you are on your own.

Questions You Should Ask

- How long has the wholesaler been in business?
- Have you (the travel agent) used them before? Were they reliable?
- WHAT IS INCLUDED IN THE PACKAGE? air, hotel, transfers, meals, room type and view, taxes—which kind, and other features—get specifics so you know what you are buying.
- When do they need your money?
- Ask for a written confirmation. Make sure what was quoted to you is spelled out in detail.
- Compare this against the final documents you receive so you can be sure you get what you paid for.
- Trip Insurance: What does this cover? How much extra does it cost? Does the wholesaler sell his own insurance?

Payments

- What are the deposit requirements? By what date do they need the payment? How much time do you have to think about it?
- How will you pay for it? Credit card is the safest.
- When is the final payment due?
- What happens if I change my mind or can't go? Find out the cancellation policy prior to paying.

Changes and Cancellations

- Any changes or cancellations can be costly, so be sure you make up your mind before giving your credit card.
- Ask about the cancellation policy. The amount of penalty you pay may depend on what day you cancel, i.e., 60 days prior, 45 days prior, 5 days prior. The closer you are to your travel dates, the more money you will lose. Sometimes insurance might cover this lost money, but not always.
- The cancellation policy is always spelled out on the legalese page of the tour brochure. Get a copy of the brochure.
- If you do change or cancel, you must do it with the confirming travel agent, not the airline or hotel.

Surfing the Web for Packages

This is a growing area. Most online travel agencies, a.k.a. travel search engines, are trying to find ways to increase their commissions, just like the travel agent. They are either developing their own system of combining travel products or are partnering up with existing websites that sell packages, i.e., *Site59.com*. Keep in mind when you are searching online for a package or tour you won't have a human being to answer any of your questions. If you need help, go to a travel agent.

For the latest information about buying packages online send an e-mail to *tips@discounttravelwisdom.com*

What Is a Travel Deal?

You would think it would be a travel component (air, hotel, etc.) that has some kind of discount or added value—a free something. But not always. Many of those "deals" are just a last-minute promotion to sell unsold travel items, seats, hotels, cars, or tours. They are usually disguised as a "package," a term that erroneously seems to mean a discount.

It can be difficult to determine whether an advertisement contains a true value. Here are a few steps to help you determine a good value:

1. Is it available for your selected dates? If not, then it's not a true value. If you are flexible and can change your dates to the dates available on the promotion, then it might be.
2. What exactly is included in the advertised rate, i.e., where in the hotel is the room located; are any features added (i.e., breakfast), are all the hotel taxes and surcharges included? Call the company running the advertisement or read the details of the online promotion.

3. Is the rate quoted cheaper than if you buy directly from the hotel, airline, etc.? Compare with web rates or call the vendor's toll-free reservations. Be sure you are comparing apples to apples, i.e., ocean-front room plus hotel taxes.
4. What is the booking and cancellation policy? Is it a "use it or lose it" promo? If your plans suddenly change, you have lost your money. Not a good value. Ditto for "a one time offer," trip valid for one specific date, or hotel.
5. Does the promotion offer you something you can't get elsewhere? Does the promo give you something for free or for a small additional amount?
6. You would then need to do a quick search to see if this promotion is a regular rate disguised as a "deal" or if you are truly getting a discount or added value, such as a free full breakfast or limo.
7. Finally, DO YOU REALLY WANT TO GO THERE? Or are you caught up in the hype of getting a discount? For example, what if there is a golf package that gives you 75% off green fees? Wow, this is great if you're a golfer. If you are NOT a golfer, this is not a value.

The only way to determine whether the advertised promotion is a good deal is to compare it to the individual components. Search the hotel or airline website or call their reservation offices and compare the available rates for the same product. Determine the extras (taxes, surcharges and fees) and add them to the air and hotel rates.

The best way to determine whether it is a good deal is to call a travel agent and book the package with them. It should cost the same unless the agent charges a well-deserved consultation fee.

Last Minute Packages and Travel Deals

Site59.com: Sells last minute PACKAGES only. Rates are quoted PER PERSON double occupancy, with a click-on link for solo travelers. Truly a last minute choice. Availability is 14 days or less prior to departure—domestic up to 3 hours prior, international 5 hours prior. All packages are nonrefundable and non-changeable. This is a good website to get last minute airfare deals if you purchase another feature such as a car rental, sightseeing tour, etc., with it.

Lastminute.com: an European website. Flight information is accessible by your country of departure. If you use the UK website, you'll only get information for London or other UK cities to Europe. If you want to originate in another country such as France, you'd have to use that website by clicking on the French flag and be proficient in reading French, as the website is in French not English. *Lastminute.com* sells airfare, hotel, packages, goods and services, theatre tickets, and restaurants. They also have an auction site.

Lowestfare.com: The website and name was purchased by *priceline.com*. It is in development for packages and cruises. Check this site periodically for new features. Also check *priceline.com* for vacation specials.

AIRLINE TOUR DESKS: Traditionally the airline tour desks offer the best value. The hotels have been fully checked out by airline staff. The airline has a reputation to uphold, so the hotels must be a minimum standard to be added to the list of hotels offered. The airfares sold, subject to availability, are "bulk airfares"—specially negotiated discounted airfares to be sold in conjunction with another feature, usually a hotel. Your ticket will only show the taxes on it.

All Inclusives: Pros and Cons

Pros

- Can be a good value if you eat 3 meals a day, drink copiously, and utilize activities and sports.
- Your only extra expenses will be for souvenirs and specialty sports (i.e., motorized sports), spa services, and other extra activities offered for a fee.
- Learn how to play tennis, wind surf or water ski. Many activities are offered to keep you entertained.
- Food is plentiful and tasty at the buffets.
- Several properties cater to families or couples.
- Generally no tipping is allowed.
- Some companies like Club Med offer a discount if you are flexible about your dates and destination. You pick the week, they pick the club and dates.

Cons

- Must be prepaid, with steep cancellation penalties.
- Some companies like Club Med have membership fees that are an additional charge.
- Several properties are for couples only. No children or single folks. Verify before you buy.
- Unlimited beverages and drinks may be included, but the line at the bar may be so long that it limits your drinking. Hard liquor may be limited to "house" brands and available only in designated areas, usually not your hotel room.
- If the airplane is a charter, then you can only get your seat assignment at check-in, probably **4 hours** prior departure, if it leaves on time. If the plane is delayed you have no option but to wait with it or buy a full ticket from another airline.
- Concierge/special services departments are either nonexistent or feeble, at best, especially over peak travel dates.
- Buffets are usually great, but with long lines. Sit-down waiter service restaurants may be disappointing and slow.

Insurance: Should You Buy It?

Trip Cancellation Insurance: If you have prepaid an expensive trip and have children, elderly or sick relatives that could cause you to abort your trip prior to or during your trip, you should buy trip cancellation insurance.

Ask your travel agent to recommend a company. They are familiar with the policies and can guide you through the rules. They will discuss with you how much insurance you need to buy to cover the extra expenses incurred, or the value of the lost portion of the trip. As with any insurance policy, read the coverage rules. Many policies do not cover "prior existing conditions." If someone has a preexisting condition, such as cancer or a cold, and an escalation of the illness occurs, you may not have coverage. Insurance also does not cover for weather delays (unless it's over 48 hours), war or terrorism.

Part Seven: Exploring Your Booking Options

Chapter 12	Exploring Your Booking Options	183
Chapter 12.1	About Travel Agents	188
Chapter 12.2	Doing It Yourself	198

CHAPTER 12

Exploring Your Booking Options

Consumer Booking Patterns

In 1973 everything in the travel business was done by telephone, telex or letter. We called the airline to make the airline reservation and hand wrote the airline ticket. Any hotel that did not have a toll-free number was requested in writing and sent via snail mail. You received a hand-typed hotel voucher as confirmation.

Most people in 1973 called a travel agent to book their travel plans. They would not even consider embarking on an overseas journey without the expertise of their local travel agent. The travel agent would book all the hotels, sell you one of two economy airfares, both refundable, and present you with a typed day-by-day itinerary. But all that has changed with the advent of computers.

In 1978, if a travel agent wanted to stay ahead of his competition, he got an airline computer system that could make airline reservations and issue "typed" airline tickets. He was considered behind the times if he sold a hand-written ticket. Eventually these airline computer systems added hotels and cars to their reservation capabilities.

By the 1990s, the systems evolved adding more and more capabilities for manipulating flight loads, pricing and availability. Eventually, the airline owners were forced out of the computer reservation business because of governmental antitrust rulings. These huge computers became independent companies and are now referred to as CRS's, Computer Reservation Systems, or GDS's, Global Distribution Systems. These GDS's developed programming that allowed them to sell computer space to other airlines, hotel companies, tour operators or anyone else willing to pay for computer storage and programming.

Somewhere in here a couple of teenagers created (in their garage) the phenomenon known as the Personal Computer or PC, for short. Back then, no one believed that everyone would own one, including IBM. Now if you don't own one, you are behind the times.

Then came the Internet, and the world of travel planning changed. And continues to change with every stroke of a typewriter key. (Huh . . . what's a typewriter?) The Internet truly put the world at your fingertips—if you could find it, that is.

Should You Do It Yourself?

"Computer Savvy" people decided they could "do it themselves"—search the Internet for travel information and deals. After all, the airlines and everyone owning a business was getting a web site. This "computer savvy" person could find anything he wanted at the cheapest price if he spent enough time digging around the net. But that has turned out to be a huge challenge. How many hours do you spend surfing and how do you know you are getting the best value for your time and money? YOU DON'T. Unless you are as experienced as a good travel agent, you probably have no idea what is a decent price for an airline seat, hotel room or car rental. Years of experience booking travel products has given the travel agent a keen eye for pricing. BUT, if you do extensive research, you may be able to "do it yourself" and get a fair price. You, just as a travel agent, might miss a sale or a better price depending on when and where you book your trip. You need to decide when enough searching is enough and accept the price at that point. The airlines have the ability to change the price of an airline ticket as many times a day as they want. They can also change the number of seats offered for sale at the lowest fare at any time (usually adding, not subtracting seats). So it is virtually impossible to find the lowest fare for your trip. (See Chapter 8, *Anatomy of an Airfare,* for description of an availability screen and corresponding airfares.) You need to decide what is a reasonable price and stick with it. This also means you need to stick to the original travel dates written on your ticket or itinerary, as a change to any portion of the ticket will incur hundreds of dollars in heavy penalties, fees and possibly additional airfare.

Know When You Are Over Your Head and Turn to a Travel Agent

You have probably spent many hours researching your trip and have mountains of papers with notes on them. Which paper has the best airline schedule, availability and price? Is the information still current? Which hotel do you like the best, which one meets your needs or is priced the lowest? Did you note the penalties attached to the reservations? Are they nonrefundable? Oops, missed that part, gotta go back and double check all the work.

Should you buy each part—air, hotel, and car—of the trip separately or as part of a prepaid package?

ARE YOU CONFUSED AND FRUSTRATED YET? If so, this may be the best time to contact a travel agent. You have an idea of what you want (from your research), and the travel agent can guide you to the best airfare, hotel and other travel products. Their advice is worth any service fee they have to charge you to stay in business. Here is what a travel agent can do for you.

What a Travel Agent Can Do for You

A travel agent can do most anything if you are willing to pay for it. Putting together travel arrangements is usually labor intensive for both the individual and the travel agent, even in this day of fax machines and emails.

Don't be put off because you have to pay a fee. In the long run, you will save money, time, and get a properly set up itinerary that meets your needs. Once you have established your guidelines and done some research, you will be in a position to determine if you can book it yourself or call a travel agent.

The most common reasons people use a travel agent are for their ability to get the best airfares and the personal service they provide. Below is a partial list of what services can be obtained from a travel agent.

General Services Provided

- Can compare airfare and hotel prices with your research information.
- Their experience and knowledge can match you to the best product for your needs.
- Find a cheaper airfare by:
  - Suggesting a different routing/connecting city.
  - Suggesting a different date of travel, time of travel, different airport.
- They have fares for most airlines.
- Can check last-seat availability on most airlines in their GDS.
- Can check the Internet for internet-only fares.
- They can see actual airplane seat maps and confirm seat assignments.
- They can confirm special meals, wheelchairs, etc.
- Can check availability for hotel, cars, tours, cruises—almost anything.
- They can help correct mistakes on tickets and reservations.
- They can assist in finding hotel rooms for difficult dates.
- They often have better hotel, car, and cruise rates, through negotiated rate contracts.
- Can offer alternatives if your choice is sold out.
- Provide written confirmation for air, car, hotel, etc. on an itinerary.
- Coordinate a business trip with a vacation.
- Can save you time and money.

This is just a basic list of what a travel agent can do for you. Every travel agent has a specialty that stands out from the multitude of services they provide. It could be selling cruises, tours, a destination or handling corporate reservations. A travel agent can do almost anything, but their experience in one area tends to stand out.

One Final Note

A travel agent is like any other professional: their opinions are based on their years of experience and knowledge. They can suggest the best components for your trip, but you ultimately are the one who has the final say. You can only hope that your collaboration with your travel agent reaps the trip you had in mind. There are limitless events that can affect the outcome of your trip. Trust that you have made the correct choices and enjoy your trip. See it as an adventure. If you want things to be perfect, you're possibly setting yourself up for a disappointment.

CHAPTER 12.1

About Travel Agents

The travel agency originated as a small business run by your neighbor's mom and dad. Modern-day trends and travel habits changed the way the local travel agency operates. To survive, the agencies started to specialize in an area of travel that was in demand in their neighborhood. It could be business/corporate travel, leisure travel, cruises or a combination of all three. Sometimes within the agency, certain people specialized in specific travel destinations, usually based on demand and personal travel experience.

Types of Travel Agencies

Business or Corporate Travel Agency

These agencies are usually located in a large city or area where there are many corporate offices. These are usually large, multi-million dollar travel agencies with offices worldwide. The agency location that handles corporate business may be located far away from the actual client. The agency communicates via toll-free numbers, emails, or fax. The services provided are specified in a contract agreement between the agency and the company. Most corporate contracts have a "management fee," otherwise known as a service fee, per transaction. The services provided usually include airline tickets, hotel reservations, and car rentals. Any other type of travel is referred to a leisure travel agent who specializes in vacation travel. This leisure agent can either be located within the agency or at another agency.

Benefits: The agency has enormous buying power and can negotiate discount contracts for airline tickets, hotels and car rentals. Often special perks are added to the agency-corporate contract. This could be free tickets based on volume, upgrades, free car coupons, or hotel stays.

Limitations: An agent in a corporate travel agency is primarily an order taker. They may be unable to suggest alternate routings or another hotel if your choice is sold out. They are trained on how to use their computer and follow the corporation's travel guidelines. They are not trained on handling problems or may be restricted from giving additional service based on the corporate contract.

The corporate travel agency may be "kicking back" all, or some, of their commission to the corporation so it is working within a very slim profit margin. They cannot afford to pay high salaries to their agents, so they tend to get inexperienced people and train them. The service a corporation gets is based on the initiative of the person they are speaking to and the training they have received from the travel agency. Don't expect them to think. They just take orders.

End Result: Often complaints of poor service reach the ears of the financial officer responsible for choosing the corporate travel agency. But money rules. If the agency has kept the travel expenses in line with the financial officer's expectations or gives a large quarterly "kickback" check, he/she would probably ignore the complaints.

For example: I once had a portion of a large corporate account. The controller selected another in-house travel agency based on the "kickback" check he received. I still dealt with a few of the top executives that wanted better service for their travel arrangements. I was continuously asked to compare airline routings and hotel prices. Almost always I was able to undercut the amount the in-house travel agency offered. It was irrelevant to the controller that the in-house corporate travel agency grossly inflated the travel volume by several million dollars. The CFO didn't care. He was able to wave a million dollar "kickback" check in the face of the chairman and say, "See what a great travel agency I selected? We saved one million dollars on travel this year by using this travel agency."

There are many ways a corporation can save on its travel budget. One is to establish caps on hotel spending by utilizing a list of suggested hotels. Another is to use the services of a full-service travel agency, not under contract, to establish competition for their travel budget. If an agency is vying for your business, they will try harder by PROVIDING SERVICE to your travelers. The service fee charged will be earned. If you use multiple travel agencies, you can easily control your travel spending by utilizing the reports from a corporate credit card such as Diners Club.

Leisure or Vacation Travel Agency

These are the agencies most people use and can be located anywhere. This is the backbone of the travel industry. Leisure bookings usually include multiple travel products, commonly prepaid. These may include airline tickets, hotel accommodations, car rentals or transfers, sightseeing, escorted tours, cruises or train tickets. A travel agent can do almost anything if you are willing to pay for their time.

Benefits: The travel agent working in a leisure agency is probably more knowledgeable about destinations and travel in general. They are detail oriented and develop relationships with vendors that have proven to be reliable and deliver a great product.

Limitations: The agent may not be as proficient on their computer and uses it only to produce an airline ticket. If the agent has limited knowledge of her computer system, you may not be getting the best price for your airline ticket, hotel reservation or car rental. They may steer you toward prepaid packages that pay them commissions, a necessity to stay in business. Hopefully, they use reputable vendors that have proven track records and deliver the product as ordered.

Sometimes a corporate travel agency may have a leisure department available as a service provided to their corporate travelers. Leisure travel is time consuming and labor intensive. Many corporate agencies have eliminated this department because they did not understand the added value it offers in spite of the extra work involved. They also have stopped offering leisure services because if something goes wrong with the trip of a top executive, the whole corporate travel account could be lost.

Group or Incentive Travel Agency

These are agencies that specialize in group travel, usually large conventions and meetings. They may, or may not, have a separate corporate department to handle ongoing corporate travel.

Benefits: One agency can work with the corporation's meeting planner and coordinate travelers' arrivals with the land arrangements. The agency negotiates the best airfare deal, makes all the individual travel arrangements, and supplies an arrival list of names to the meeting coordinator or ground supplier.

Limitations: The agency is working with quick reservations and high volume with small profit. Details, like frequent flyer numbers, seating preference or special meal requests can get screwed up, or not done at all. The agency does not want to add services or make changes, as this increases costs dramatically.

An incentive travel agency puts together a brochure with various prizes that can be offered to employees as an incentive to produce higher sales. The top producers win the trip offered. This can be an individual trip where you can travel at any time, or a company-sponsored trip for specific dates and destinations with all expenses paid.

Types of Travel Agents

Corporate Travel Agent: These are salaried employees who are trained to handle business travelers. They must be proficient in using their computer system, as most of the information they work with is stored there. Some of the information the agent accesses is the individual traveler's profile and the corporation's travel guidelines—who can travel first or business class, which hotels to stay in, and special airfare deals and contracts. The agent only knows how to check availability for flights, hotels and cars. They are not trained in travel consulting or destination knowledge. They are primarily order takers. If you find one that goes the extra step or has added knowledge, you are lucky.

Leisure or Vacation Travel Agent: These usually are salaried employees who are destination specialists. Their business is built on knowledge, personal travel experience, and service. Their knowledge and expertise can match you to the best travel product for your vacation guidelines. Look for a travel agent that has been to your destination and has some kind of industry credential such as CTC—Certified Travel Counselor or MCC—Master Cruise Counsellor.[3]

Independent Contractor/Commission Agent: This travel agent receives a commission rather than a salary for any travel booked. This agent may be

[3] This is the way each program identifies itself. CTC—Certified Travel Counselor and MCC—Master Cruise Counsellor.

on site at the travel agency or work from home with a computer link to the host travel agency. Since their income is derived from your purchase, they have an incentive to find you the best product for your money. They tend to be extremely knowledgeable and service oriented.

Homebased Travel Agent: As a result of the airlines discontinuing commissions, more and more travel agents are working out of their homes to reduce overhead. This agent can be an independent contractor with a tie to a host travel agency or full-service travel agency located in someone's home. Some have an office set up in their home where they can meet with clients. Others do business strictly by telephone. Either way, they are usually extremely knowledgeable in one particular area, such as cruises or European travel. They have traveled extensively, taken training courses to update their skills and knowledge, and are service oriented.

What Kind of Travel Agent Do You Need?

If you are searching for a travel agent without a recommendation, first determine what kind of agent you are looking for. Unless you are traveling on business, you would want to find a leisure or vacation travel agent, not a corporate travel agent. They have different training and knowledge.

When you call them, tell them you are looking for a travel agent to build a relationship with and that you have a few questions. Tell them you also have a trip in mind and would like their help planning it.

What is the agent's specialty? Do they only sell cruises or adventure travel? How long have they been leisure travel agents? Do they have any industry credentials? What training have they received? Have they traveled to your destination recently? How often do they update their knowledge and computer skills? Are computer skills important to you? Do they use the Internet? These are some of the questions you can ask the travel agent.

Although most travel agents can handle any kind of travel request, you want to find a travel agent experienced in your destination. ICTA—Institute of Certified Travel Agents—has a list of people who have taken one of their Destination Specialist courses, see, *icta.com*. If you are taking a cruise, find an agent who has the MCC—Master Cruise Counsellor—certification. Not only will they have added expertise in selling cruises, they may also have access to discounts not offered elsewhere. You can find a list of MCC's at *cruising.org*.

How to Find a Reliable Travel Agent

This can be a challenge. Here are a few suggestions:

Recommendation From a Friend: First, I would start with a recommendation from someone you know, who has the same tastes and budget as you, and whose judgment you trust. Most travel agents get their business from referrals. If the agent provides adequate service and makes a client happy, the client will probably return and buy again, and refer everyone they know. Start here.

Recommendation From Your Corporate Travel Agency: If your company has an agreement with a corporate travel agency, you may want to call them and ask who handles vacation travel. Usually they have a list of people to refer you to. These vacation agents are usually very good. If they do not give you the service you want, it reflects back on the referring corporate agency and could jeopardize the corporate relationship.

Travel Industry Recommendations: Several organizations have lists of travel agents that have invested time and money to earn credentials that establish them as professional, knowledgeable and dedicated agents. Much time and money is invested in the training classes offered by the following organizations:

- ICTA—Institute of Certified Travel Agents—*www.icta.com*: This organization offers the most intensive travel training programs in the industry. They offer several certification programs with two main levels of certification: CTA—Certified Travel Associate, or the more advanced, CTC—Certified Travel Counselor. Agents who display these credentials have studied and been tested on various subjects about running a travel agency, working with clients, sales techniques, and destination background. The agents will carry the letters CTA or CTC after their name, like me: Elaine Ktistes, CTC.
- ICTA also offers Destination Specialist courses and lists agents who have been tested and proven knowledgeable in various destinations. Visit their website *www.icta.com* for a list.

- CLIA—Cruise Line International Association, *www.cruising.org*. Any travel agency can be a member of the association by paying dues. You want to look for a travel agent who has taken the cruise training course and has become a Master Cruise Counsellor. They would carry the letters MCC or ACC after their name.
- ASTA—American Society of Travel Agents, *www.astanet.com*. ASTA offers its members various courses on how to sell travel. ASTA is an industry association that promotes professionalism and a code of ethics. Members display the ASTA logo. There is no testing or monitoring of the skills of the agents in an ASTA member agency. Call an agency, tell them you are looking for a travel agent, and ask lots of questions. See the following section on your local travel agency.

Your Local Travel Agency: When you walk in the door, announce to whomever you speak to that you are looking for a travel agent and would like to speak to someone familiar with your destination. This will get their attention. Have your guidelines ready.

Visit them and see if they look professional. Are you greeted immediately when you walk in? Are there brochures available? Is the office neat and attractive? Do they have computers? Look at the windows and see if they have any industry logos displayed, i.e., ASTA, CLIA. Be wary of airline stickers on the door. Any reputable agency won't bother to clutter up windows with these. Speak to someone and ask about their experience, training, and certifications. Ask them if there is an agent you can speak to that is an expert in your destination. Until you develop a relationship with them, only pay by credit card (and within 60 days of departure) and get a receipt or invoice specifying what you have purchased.

Via the Internet: This may be extremely chancy. You have no way of knowing whether the person you are dealing with is legitimate or not. Use an online travel agency with extreme caution. This includes the mega online sites like *orbitz.com*, *cheaptickets.com*, *travelocity.com*, *expedia.com*, or anyone else. If you decide to use an online agency other that the mega well-known ones, verify the credentials of the agency or agent. Most reputable agencies will be members of ASTA or CLIA. A reputable agent will have a certification designation such as CTA, CTC from ICTA or ACC or MCC from CLIA. Call ASTA and verify whether the travel agency is truly a member.

And, most importantly, only pay by credit card and receive a written invoice stating what you have specifically paid for. If you pay by check, you could lose your money.

www.travants.com: This is a potentially useful website. This is a new website designed to find a travel agent. Agents apply, pay a fee and are interviewed about their travel knowledge and experience. Once accepted, agents are listed by destination specialty: Caribbean, Europe, Asia, etc. Read through the bios and chose one that has the experience you need. As stated before, pay by credit card and receive a written invoice detailing what you have purchased.

Getting a Good Deal

If you have done your research for your trip and called and questioned your new travel agent, trust that they will find you the best value for your dollar. Although experience and service vary widely, the agency wants you to come back. They will do their best to meet your needs and your price. From vast experience, travel agencies establish relationships with specific vendors that provide good value and good service. Travel agents develop these relationships so they'll get a preferred commission rate, have a reliable product to sell, and have a name of a person to go to if help is needed with a problem.

Service Fees

Service fees vary from agent to agent, request to request. It can be a fee for an airline ticket or a planning fee for an extensive itinerary. The reason service fees are more prevalent is that the airlines have eliminated paying commission on airline tickets. What was once a lucrative business, now barely covers the rent. For example, in 1995, prior to the beginning of the reduction in airline commissions, if you purchased a first-class domestic ticket for $4000, the commission was about $375. Now that same ticket pays no commission. The agent has to find a way to offset the huge loss of $375. The travel agent has moved from selling airline tickets to selling services. They have always provided the service for free but now, out of necessity, they have to charge you for their time and experience.

In this age of the Internet, many computer-literate people might be lured into doing "it" themselves. You need to know when this is appropriate and when it is advisable to get help from an expert.

My Service Fees

All of my service fees vary depending on the complexity of the request and the time involved. Some are standard, as is the ticket transaction fee. **WHEN YOU BUY ONLY AN AIRLINE TICKET THIS FEE COVERS:**

- Trip consultation, advice on routing, finding the best fare, suggesting alternatives
- My time and knowledge processing the computer transactions
- Special services needed, such as seat assignments, special meals, wheelchairs or any special assistance required
- Creating an itinerary which includes check-in instructions
- Printing the paper documents, i.e., ticket receipt and invoice
- Mailing or delivery
- Computer and office expense
- Watching over your itinerary for any changes
- Problem solving if necessary.

A $50 per ticket fee barely covers these expenses. I consider it a "loss leader," someday hoping you will book a more expensive trip or refer someone else who will.

Sample Fees

■ Per ticket processing fee	$ 50 each
■ Reissue fee	100 each and up
■ Itinerary planning fee, simple	150 each and up
■ Itinerary planning fee, complex	300 each and up
■ Frequent flyer tickets	100 each and up plus a fee for the time spent processing
■ In-person consultation fee	**300 per hour***
■ Time wasted on hold for wholesaler	**300 per hour***

There are many other services that I charge for that are not listed here. Miscellaneous services are priced according to time involved, difficulty of transaction, and monies paid on your behalf.

*Please be aware that the higher fees are to deter people from shopping and wasting my time. I make no money giving free information. And, while I'm doing that, I am unable to process trips for people who have already paid me. It stops me from earning a living. My advice: Establish your guidelines and do some research prior to calling the travel agent. It will have you focused and ready to ask the questions you really need answers to.

If you would like to use my company's services, go to my website: *discounttravelwisdom.com* and fill out the preplanning form. There is a fee of $50 to process your request. An experienced travel agent will review it, and if accepted, will forward it on to a destination specialist to handle your booking. Not all requests can be fulfilled. If your request is accepted, the $50 referral fee is nonrefundable and not applied to your trip.

CHAPTER 12.2
Doing It Yourself

Steps For Doing It Yourself

The process for researching by phone or online is basically the same. For online suggestions and website recommendations, see the individual chapters, *Surf the Web for Airfares,* cars or hotels.

1. **Establish Your Guidelines,** first choice and second, see Part 1, *Preplanning,* for detailed instructions.
2. **Call or Check Online with the Various Airlines Serving Your Airport.** Unless you know which one flies nonstop to your destination, you have to call around or check several websites to find out. If an airline does not have nonstop flights, chose an airline with the most direct routing via their hub/connecting city. Avoid the airline with a "hub" that is not in a direct path. You might pay more money to go out of your way. Airfares are loosely based on the air miles flown. Theoretically, the longer the flight, the higher the price. If researching online, be sure to load the *Sidestep.com* plug-in and do a quick search there. See the chapter, *Understanding the Airline Industry.*
3. **Check the Availability** of the least expensive airfare, usually a nonrefundable airfare. This is where pricing gets tricky and time consuming. Are there cheaper airfares on alternate dates, flights, airlines, or routing?
4. **Book Your Airline Reservation, but Do Not Pay For It Yet.** Obtain reservation/confirmation number. This may not be possible if booking online.
5. **Review Booked Itinerary.** If you have access to email or a fax machine, obtain a written confirmation and READ IT IMMEDI-

ATELY. If you do not have access to a fax machine or computer, or if the airline cannot fax it to you, call the airline back and give your confirmation number to a new reservation agent. Have them read back what your confirmation says. AND LISTEN. Write down on a separate piece of paper what this person told you. Hopefully the information is the same. If not, change it and repeat the process.

6. **Verify the Rules of Your Airfare.** You cannot change your ticket without incurring high penalty fees. Most of the airlines have raised the reissue fee to $100 per ticket. If you change your outbound flight, you have to start over with the pricing. The outbound price is based on how far in advance you purchase your ticket, the fare and availability in existence at that time. Generally, the closer you are to your departure date, the higher the airfare. Also note that the new nonrefundable rules require you to make changes prior to the date written on your ticket. If you don't, your ticket has no value.
7. You must **Purchase Your Ticket Within 24 Hours** or by the date or time the agent told you to, possibly the same day. The airfare is not locked in/guaranteed until you purchase your ticket. It can change within minutes of making your reservation. It is essential that you have all your guidelines in place and have done your hotel and car research too. Do not buy your airline ticket until you have booked your hotel room (but do not prepay it until your airline ticket is set). You will be doing a lot of back and forth research until you get the confirmations you want. If you purchase a package, your airline ticket and hotel arrangements are paid for at the same time.
8. **Cancel Any Duplicate Reservations You Made** or you could be billed for them.
9. **Proceed to the Next Portion of Your Itinerary:** Unless you bought a package, the next important step is checking hotel availability. See detailed instructions in the hotel chapters. Do not pay for your hotel until air arrangements are set.
10. **Process Car Rental and Other Components of Your Trip.**
11. If you are frustrated or confused, now may be the time to call a travel agent. See Chapter 12.1, *About Travel Agents* for help in finding one.

Part Eight: What to Do After You Buy Your Ticket

Chapter 13	Travel Documents	203
Chapter 13.1	Airport Check-In Procedures	205

CHAPTER 13

Travel Documents

Wow! You have finally finished booking your travel arrangements. Whether you booked the whole trip online or with a travel agent, you need to review all documents as soon as you get them. Be sure to check the spelling of all names and see that they match the government-issued identification you will use at check in. Also verify that the dates are correct. Do this within 24 hours of making your reservations. If you wait to look at your documents in the car on the way to the airport, it will be too late to fix any mistake. You may have to buy a new expensive ticket to replace it.

Put your documents in a safe place until you need them on your departure date.

Document Check List

- VALID GOVERNMENT PICTURE IDENTIFICATION: See Chapter 1 for types
- AIRLINE TICKET RECEIPT: either a paper ticket or proof of electronic ticket, such as an itinerary or confirmation number
- Itinerary. This should be as detailed as possible. It should contain flight information with your electronic ticket confirmation number, hotel addresses and phone numbers, along with dates

and confirmation numbers. Leave one at home with a trusted friend, pack one in your suitcase and another in your carry-on bag
- Package, tour or cruise documents
- Hotel documents and/or confirmation numbers
- Car rental confirmation number
- Driver's license, especially if you are renting a car
- Credit Cards
- Membership identification: AAA, AARP, frequent flyer numbers
- Passport, if you are traveling internationally
- Foreign country visa stamp if applicable (see Chapter 1, *Types of Documentation*)

Other Stuff Check List

- Money: cash, travelers checks or local currency
- Copy of passport, itinerary with ticket numbers, copy of travelers checks. Leave with a trusted friend
- Emergency contacts list
- Insurance information—medical, homeowners and car
- Baggage tags on all bags
- Medication and copy of prescriptions
- If you are taking valuables with you, make a list and take pictures of them. Leave list at home
- Guidebooks and index cards with your research information on them
- Camera, extra camera battery, and film

Packing Tips

- If you are carrying medications, be sure to put them in your carry-on bag or purse. Also include a copy of the prescription with you. It will eliminate any hassles while you are going through security or customs.
- The new machines used to scan checked luggage will destroy film. Do not pack film inside checked luggage but pack it in your carry-on bag. Remove film from packaging and put it in a clear plastic bag.
- The new security rules require you to check your bags WITHOUT LOCKING THEM. Do not pack anything valuable unless you don't mind it disappearing.

CHAPTER 13.1

Airport Check-In Procedures

Running the Check-In Gauntlet

Since September 11th, 2001, travel has been forever changed. The use of airplanes as attack missiles on the World Trade Center and the Pentagon have made it necessary to change the way Americans travel. Someday, the U.S. Government will figure out the best way to handle security at our airports. Until then, here are some tips for dealing with airport personnel.

Airline Ticket Counter Check In

- Arrive at the airport at least 1½ hours prior to flight departure. Double-check with your airline for their specific check-in policy.
- Murphy's law: if you are running late, hit a lot of traffic, etc., the line at the ticket counter will have 200 people in it. Plan your time accordingly. The reverse is also true. If you arrive at the airport 2 or more hours prior to flight departure, the entire check-in process, from standing in line at the ticket counter through security to the gate, will take you only 15 minutes.
- If the airline offers curbside check-in and the line is short, check in there. If you need to change anything on your reservation or have a paper ticket, you should go to the long check-in line inside the terminal.
- Have all your travel documents readily available. Carry them on your person or in your carry-on bag. Do not pack your documents inside your suitcase.

- When you reach the agent at the ticket counter, you must present your government-issued identification along with your electronic ticket itinerary or paper ticket. This will make it easier for the agent to find your reservation. If you have an electronic ticket, the minimum you should have is the reservation number/record locator.
- At the ticket counter, the agent will take your bag and attach a destination baggage tag. Look at the tag and make sure it has the city name of your final destination (Not the connecting city). The agent will give you your boarding pass. On it will be the gate number and boarding time. You must be in the gate area by the time indicated on your boarding pass.
- You will then go to the security area to get to your gate. Only ticketed passengers with boarding passes are allowed through here.

Tips

- Verify in advance **how many bags** you can check in and how much carry-on is allowed. The airlines are no longer as generous as in the past. They see overweight baggage as a major source of extra income. The free baggage allowance is being reduced by approximately 25%—a previous 70 pound limit now is subject to excess baggage charges when over 50 pounds.
- **Have baggage tags** on all your bags, including carry- on. Put minimal information on the tag. You want the airline to be able to reach you if they find it, but you don't want a thief to know you're not at home. Your name and telephone number should be enough.
- **Mark your suitcase** in a way that is readily identifiable. I once used green masking tape to form my initials on a large hard-sided bag.
- **Bring reading material** to occupy yourself in line and at the gate area. Bring **games for the kids**. Make sure they are quiet games, no buzzing, or binging. This goes for cell phones too.
- **Pack a lunch:** If your trip is an all-day event, you may want to bring along a lunch or snack foods. The airlines are eliminating most food, and what they might serve is woefully inadequate. A TV dinner has more food (and is more nourishing). Many fast-food restaurants are popping up in big city airports.
- **Do not buy expensive luggage.** This will alert thieves to grab your bags. They may think there is more expensive stuff inside.

- **Never pack anything inside your suitcase that you can't afford to lose.** Assume it might be lost. Do not pack valuables. Don't bring any expensive jewelry or gadgets. You will be very disappointed when they disappear.
- If you are taking a long journey, you may want to **pack a set of clothing in your carry-on bag**.
- **Cell phone courtesy** and safety: Please make all phone calls prior reaching the airport. People around you do not want to hear phones ringing nor want to listen to loud one-sided conversations. Cell phones must be turned off once you enter the aircraft.

AUTHOR'S NOTE

TO CELL PHONE USERS: Using a cell phone on an airplane can possibly get you a two-year prison sentence (in the UK anyway). A cell phone can interfere with navigation aboard an aircraft, hence the restriction. The crew (and fellow passengers) will advise you to turn them off and leave them off. For your safety and your fellow traveler's, I suggest you adhere to the crew's directions. Be aware of people around you too, when you use your cell phone on the ground.

Airport Security Tips

This subject fuels many news stories about the ineptness of the U.S. Government and airport security. Unfortunately, the stories may be true. Bite your lip and trudge on through. Here are some tips to make it easier:

- Have valid government identification handy. You will, again, have to present it. See Chapter 1 for types of documentation.
- Wear slip-on shoes. If you are selected by airport security for a "personal inspection" you may be asked to take off your footwear. Sneakers are a major target. They do provide a chair for you to sit

in and do this. If you wear slip-on shoes, i.e., loafers, this process would be easier.

- If you are "randomly" selected to be "hand searched" agree to this without complaining. (Yes, I do know how hard this is.) The officers are only doing a job they are trained to do. Whether it works or not is irrelevant.
- BE AWARE OF LAPTOP THIEVES: Pack laptop computers in a case that can be easily opened. You will have to take your laptop out of its case to have it inspected. Make sure the person in front of you has cleared the security doorway before putting your laptop on the belt. Many laptops have been stolen from the security belt by a team of people blocking your passage through the security doorway. Your laptop goes through the security camera and sits on the belt waiting for you to pass through the security doorway and pick it up. Someone in front of you picks it up and takes off with it while you're waiting your turn to walk through the security doorway.

Gate Check In

Once you have cleared security, proceed to your gate. The gate number is written on your boarding pass and was pointed out to you by the ticket counter agent. Find a seat and listen for the boarding instructions. Generally, boarding starts 30 minutes prior to departure for domestic flights, and 45–60 minutes prior for international flights. If you don't hear your row or group number called, go to the gate agent by the ramp doorway and hand her your boarding pass. All people must be onboard at least 10 minutes prior to departure. This policy may vary by airline.

Tips

- Again, there is a random security check as you pass into the gangway. Have your identification handy.
- If you wander around the gate area, be back at the gate by the boarding time written on your boarding pass.
- Do not leave your bags unattended. They may disappear—either stolen or removed by security.

- If you buy anything from the duty-free shops, be sure to get your boarding pass back from them. (They need your name and flight number for your purchase.)
- Please follow boarding instructions. People are boarded in a specific order, first and business class first, then the back of the economy section to the front of the economy section. This is done to keep people and baggage from blocking the aisle and to speed up the boarding process.
- Place your carry-on bag in the overhead bin over your seat, not another, or under your seat. Do not place your bags in the overhead bin in the front of the plane. This space is reserved for the people sitting in the seats beneath.
- If you have too much carry-on or arrive too late to find storage space, your bags may be taken from you and checked in. The flight attendant will give you a luggage receipt. Your bags will appear in the gangway as you walk off the plane. Look for them there, not in the baggage claim area.

Car Rental Check In

Where you check in at the airport depends on whether the car company has a check-in counter in the baggage claim area or only a shuttle bus that takes you to an offsite location. If you don't see a check-in counter, or if you don't want to check in at the counter in the baggage claim area, go outside and look for the car rental bus area. There is usually a designated area for shuttle buses to stop. Finding this area may be a bit of a challenge. Look for signs that point to ground transportation or shuttle bus pick up. Or ask someone who looks like they work at the airport for directions. The shuttle buses for the larger companies tend to circle the airport terminals every few minutes. You may have to call smaller companies to be picked up.

Tips

- Have a reservation. Finding a car rental at the last minute can be costly.
- Be familiar with the rate confirmed, car size and extra day rate. Compare this to what you actually get.

- Have a credit card with at least $500 available credit on it. Occasionally, the car company may hold the value of the car against your credit card. Usually they hold the amount estimated on your rental contract. Do not use debit cards.
- Be familiar with your insurance coverage. Know what coverage is included with your credit card, corporate discount program, or personal car insurance. This way you will be armed with information when an unsavory counter agent tries to coerce you into buying unneeded insurance.
- Consider buying liability insurance if you do not have it on your own car's insurance. See the car rental chapter for detailed information about car insurance.

Part Nine: Rules, Changes, Refunds

Chapter 14 What to Do If You Can't Go 213

CHAPTER 14

What to Do If You Can't Go

See the separate sections for changing regular, full-fare tickets.

If you did your preplanning steps as laid out in the front of this book, you probably have nailed down your plans and will not need this section. But as Murphy once said . . . stuff happens. Unforeseen circumstances have ruined the best-laid plans. Below are some guidelines for handling changes to your trip.

I will repeat here the rules of a nonrefundable fare, as this is one of the most important points I can make in this book

Basic Rules for Nonrefundable Tickets

Most of the common nonrefundable airfares are governed by the same general tariff rulings. See Chapter 8.2 for a detailed explanation. They usually include:

- **Nonrefundable**—you can NEVER get your money back.
- **Changes Must Be Done Prior to the Date Printed on Your Ticket.**
- **Reissue/Change Fee**—is generally $100. The "no frills" airlines charge different amounts.
- **Advance Purchase Requirements**—can be 7, 14, 21, 30 days. Usually the further in advance you purchase your ticket, the cheaper the airfare.
- **Minimum/Maximum Stay**—Normally a Saturday night stay is the minimum, 30 days is the maximum. Again, ask. It may vary depending on the routing or fare rule.
- **Limited Inventory**—There are several nonrefundable categories on every plane. A certain percentage of seats are allotted to each "bucket" or category. When the lowest fare "bucket" is sold out, the next higher fare available could be confirmed. See Chapter 8.2, *Anatomy of an Airfare.*
- **Roundtrip Purchase**—Certain markets with heavy demand may offer one-way nonrefundable fares. Also, most "no frills" airlines sell one-way nonrefundable airfares.
- **Use the Same Airline Roundtrip.**
- **24-Hour Ticketing Rule** (see explanation in Chapter 8.2).

Making Changes to Nonrefundable Tickets

A fact of life in the travel business is that people WILL alter their plans. Unfortunately, this can be costly. Most discount airline tickets or prepaid packages are subject to hefty penalties for changing or canceling. Rarely can you get a refund. Here are some guidelines:

Have This Information Available

- **Does Your Ticket Allow for Changes?** Some airfares are good only for the specific flight purchased. If you got your ticket from a bidding site such as *priceline.com* your ticket CANNOT be changed.
- **What Is the Airline Penalty Charge?** Usually $100 for a domestic ticket unless it's a "no frills" airline.
- **What Is the Fare on Your Ticket?** Do not include any ticketing fees or service charges from your travel agent or website.
- **Do You Have an Electronic Ticket or a Paper Ticket?**

- **How Did You Purchase Your Ticket?** Online, by phone with the airline, through a travel agent?
- **How Did You Pay for Your Ticket?** Hopefully by credit card. If you paid by cash, check, or airline voucher, you must go in person to the agency or airline and work with them.

Where to Change Your Ticket

Changing an airline ticket is very complicated. There are many components, and too many things can go wrong. It is best that you speak to a trained person rather than relying on a computer program. If you bought your ticket from a travel agent, go to them. If you bought online, call their customer service toll-free number. Otherwise, call the airline.

How to Change a Nonrefundable Ticket

The following information applies to changing the *outbound flight or the entire ticket*. See the following section for changing the return flight only.

- *YOU MUST CHANGE YOUR TICKET PRIOR TO THE DATE PRINTED ON YOUR TICKET. OTHERWISE YOU HAVE FORFEITED YOUR TICKET.*
- Have your confirmation number available.
- Is everyone in your party changing?
- Have your new dates and times at hand.
- Have your valid credit card ready.
- Call the airline, online customer service, or travel agent. Tell them you want to change your ticket.
- Give them your reservation number. They will display your reservation and review what you are currently holding.
- Make the new reservation for your new dates. This is where things can get tricky. Are your new dates available at the original price? Does the original fare still exist?
- What is the price of the new reservation? Does this price make sense? What was the price of the original ticket? Subtract this price from the new price. Is the amount more than the original ticket? Is it less? Add the $100 airline penalty fee to this amount. This is what your credit card will be charged.

AUTHOR'S NOTE **Tip!** Before changing your current reservation, call the airline and get a quote for a new reservation for your new dates/flights. Do not tell them you have an existing reservation. Sometimes the GDS or airline computer can quote the wrong fare on an old reservation because it is reading an old, invisible computer creation date. Few reservation agents are aware of this and may quote you a much higher airfare if they are working from your original reservation.

Original ticket price:	$294.00
New ticket price	–314.00
Difference	+ 20.00
Add penalty fee	+100.00
Pay this amount	$120.00

Please note, to make this change, you are now paying a total of $414: the new itinerary is $314 PLUS the penalty fee of $100. You have made 2 payments: $294 plus $120.

- You probably won't have the 24 hours to make a decision. **It Will Be "Instant Purchase."**
- **Give Your Credit Card Number** for the additional amount due. Some airlines require you to use the same card as on the original ticket. Once you give your credit card number, you are committed for the new reservation. Any more changes will incur more fees.
- **Ask for the Reservation Number.** It should be the same if your ticket was an electronic ticket. If it was a paper ticket, it may or may not be the same.
- **As for a Faxed or E-mailed Itinerary to Review, as Soon as You Get It.** If you don't look at it until you're in the car on the way to the airport, it may be too late to fix a mistake. If you find an error, call the airline or travel agent immediately.

Changing the Return Flight of a Nonrefundable Ticket

Please read the section above for changing the outbound portion of a nonrefundable ticket. Most of the same information applies.

- What are the minimum and maximum stay requirements for your airfare?
- Is your airfare valid for only certain days of the week?
- Is your airfare valid for only specific flight times?
- What letter/inventory is the return flight on your ticket confirmed in? (It's okay if you don't know this.)
- Was the original fare a published roundtrip fare, or was it two one-way nonrefundable airfares on one ticket?
- How much did you pay for your airline ticket?
- How much is the penalty fee?

All of these questions have an impact on the price of your new ticket. The best way to change the return flight is to call the airline and do it over the phone.

THE NEW CARDINAL RULE OF CHANGING NONREFUNDABLE TICKETS: YOU MUST MAKE YOUR CHANGE PRIOR TO THE DATE PRINTED ON YOUR TICKET OR YOU WILL FORFEIT THE PRICE YOU PAID.

If the Flight You Want Is Sold Out, What Do You Do?

Prior to the date printed on your ticket, call the airline or your travel agent to change your ticket. There are too many variables, and you need an expert's help to do this correctly. The person will review your itinerary and go over your fare. Then they will search for a flight that fits your new date and price. If the inventory is sold out, the next higher fare level available will be offered. Sometimes it may only be an additional $10. You might want to pay this in order to get your choice.

- You cannot change the cities written on your ticket. If you do, you will need to reissue the entire ticket and pay the new price plus the penalty fee, even if you are not changing the outbound flight.
- The new reservation must be booked in the same inventory as written on your ticket. Otherwise you may pay considerably more money, or even have to buy a new ticket.

Once you have found a flight that works for you, change your reservation by phone.

Changes for Other Than Nonrefundable Tickets

- Verify the rules of the ticket.
- If there is no penalty attached to the airfare, call the airline or travel agent and have them book the new flight.
- If your new airfare is the same as the original fare, your new flight will be matched up to your electronic ticket.
- If your new airfare is not the same, the original ticket will be electronically refunded (refund message sent via computer), and a new ticket will be issued. You will see two items on your credit card: one will be a credit for the first ticket; the second will be a charge for the new ticket.

AUTHOR'S NOTE

If you have extenuating circumstances (like a death in the immediate family), you can send the original nonrefundable ticket—not a copy, get an electronic ticket printed out (pay paper ticket fee)—with a letter to the airline's customer relations/service department. Request a refund. Or ask for a "transportation voucher" that is transferable to another person. This way you can "assign it"/sell it to another person other than the name on the original ticket. As with everything regarding airline tariff rules, it depends on whom you talk to and what their authority is. An airport ticket counter agent might have more leverage to help you than a reservation agent.

Also note, there are many markets that have advanced purchase fares that have no penalty attached. They only have an advance purchase requirement and limited inventory. If this inventory is sold out or you are less that the advance purchase date rule, i.e., you're changing your ticket 2-days prior to departure and the fare requires you to change it 3-days in advance, you will have to buy a new one and refund the old one.

Refunding Full-Fare Tickets

- Are you sure your ticket does not have a penalty attached to it?
- Did you pay by credit card, or something else?

If you have a full-fare ticket, one that does not have a penalty fee attached to it, you can get a full refund.

If you purchased online or by phone, the unused ticket will stay in most airline's electronic ticket database for a month and then will automatically be refunded by the computer. But don't count on this happening automatically. As soon as you know you will not be traveling, call the airline or travel agent and request that the ticket be refunded immediately. Otherwise, you may forget you have an unused ticket sitting in the airline's computer. It could stay there forever, and you just donated $650 to the airline!

- If you paid for your ticket by cash or check, call or take it back to where you purchased it. They should give you a full refund, probably in the form of a check.
- If you paid by credit card and the travel agency/company has gone out of business, you should be able to get a refund from the airline if the ticket was reported in the agency's weekly sales report. If not, call your credit card company and request a refund under the Fair Credit Act Bill.
- If the travel agency/company you bought your ticket from has gone out of business and you paid by cash or check, send your ticket by *certified mail* directly to the refund department at the airline, or take it in person to their ticket counter. Getting a refund this way is a bit difficult because they do not know who paid for the original ticket. If you have a cancelled check for the ticket, send a copy along. If the travel agency had reported your ticket in its weekly accounting to ARC, Airlines Reporting Corp., you should be able to get a refund from the airline. If the travel agency/company did not pay for your ticket, then you are out of luck.

The Refund Process

- If you paid by credit card, they will credit the ORIGINAL credit card printed on the ticket, probably in 4–8 weeks.
- The length of time a refund takes depends on your credit card statement's closing date and the date that the airline sends its computer message to the credit card company. Normally this is done weekly. If you purchased your ticket from a travel agency, add a few weeks because they first report the refund to ARC, once a week, who then forwards the refund to the airline and, eventually, on to the credit card company.
- If you paid by check (a REAL NO-NO), the airline ticket counter will possibly issue a check upon presentation of an ID that matches the name on the ticket. This gets into a real sticky area of fraud. Refund rules will depend on whom you are speaking with.
- If you paid by check through a travel agency, they will either send you a check or hold a credit in your account for future use.

Part Ten: How To's for Frequent Flyers

Chapter 15 Frequent Flyer Miles 223

CHAPTER 15

Frequent Flyer Miles

What Are Frequent Flyer Miles?

"Miles," in this case, refer to the credits or points you can collect by following the rules of the "program." These programs have created such customer loyalty that you will find them everywhere, but the biggest ones are the airline programs; hence the name "frequent flyer miles."

- ***If you focus your buying and traveling choices to one common program, you can quickly earn enough "miles" to redeem for airline tickets, hotel rooms, car rentals, gifts, or donations to charitable organizations.***

Using frequent flyer miles is the best way to maximize your savings and get the best value for your dollar.

How to Accrue/Collect Miles

Because of their popularity and customer loyalty, airline frequent flyer programs have expanded the ways to collect miles/points. The first thing you need to do is to:

- ***Join one or two of the airline frequent flyer programs.***

Based on the airport you regularly fly out of, chose one or two airlines, enroll in their frequent flyer programs, and concentrate flying on them whenever you travel.

Or you may first want to decide where you want to go on vacation and then enroll in the airline that flies there (assuming they serve your local airport). Concentrate your flying and buying with the airline that you most likely will travel on. Do not depend on airline frequent flyer partners because the airlines may not be partners next year. For that matter, don't depend on the airline that currently flies there to be in business or still flying to your destination a year from now. The airlines are constantly revising their list of partners and the cities they fly to.

- ***Obtain an airline credit card that collects frequent flyer miles.***

Airline Credit Card Programs: Every airline has a credit card program that accrues mileage for money spent. If you do not travel often enough to accrue miles by flying, you can add to your mileage by using a credit card issued by an airline. Verify that you get one mile (or more) for every dollar spent, and verify the interest rate if you carry a balance. Beware the interest rate can be an outrageous 22 percent!! If possible, pay off your balance monthly.

Also note, certain airline credit cards periodically offer bonus miles if you are a "good customer" or when they are running promos. Watch your statement or newsletter insert.

American Express Cards: MEMBERSHIP MILES, 1-800-AXP-EARN, *www.americanexpress.com.* You accrue "membership miles" for every dollar you charge to your card. It depends on the airline or hotel whether your one membership mile is redeemable for one mile on that airline or hotel. Verify first. Also, the list of participating airlines changes periodically. As of this writing, the following airlines participate and give you one point per dollar spent: Continental, Delta, Frontier, US Airways, Southwest, Hawaiian. International airlines are: Aer Lingus, Air France, Air Jamaica, Alitalia, All Nippon, Aeromexico, Cathay Pacific, El AL, Mexicana, Latinpass, Qantas, South African Airways, SWISS, and Virgin Atlantic.

There are several types of AMEX cards with different promotions. Verify what your card includes. With several of the cards, you must enroll in the Membership Miles program (this is separate from establishing a credit card account) and pay a $40 fee to activate the mileage program. They are the Personal Amex card, Gold card, and the Small business card. Corporate GREEN cards cost $75 to enroll. PLATINUM and other premium AMEX Cards have no extra fee to join Membership Miles. You are automatically enrolled.

Diners Club Card: Club Rewards Program, *www.dinersclubus.com,* 1-800-234-4034 . You are automatically enrolled. No separate fee. The list of participants is extensive: Aer Lingus, Air Canada, Air France, Alaskan, American, America West, Asiana, British Airways, Continental, Delta, El Al, Frontier, Hawaiian, Icelandair, Korean, Latinpass, Mexicana, Midwest Express, Northwest, SAS, South African Airways, Southwest, Thai, United, US Airways, and Virgin Atlantic.

Obviously with all these airline choices, this credit card is my preferred choice. There is no fee to accrue miles, but they can take at least 2 to 3 weeks to transfer miles to your airline, so plan ahead.

AUTHOR'S NOTE

The name on the airline ticket must exactly match the name on the frequent flyer account to accrue mileage. Just because you paid for someone else's ticket does not entitle you to accrue mileage on their ticket. If you used a credit card that accrues miles, you will get the dollar value of the ticket as miles on your account. Also, you cannot use someone else's frequent flyer number; the name on the ticket and the frequent flyer account must match. You cannot fly and use your brother's frequent flyer number.

Other Ways to Accrue Frequent Flyer Miles

The best suggestion I can give you is to call your airline and ask them how to collect miles. The list could be extensive. Promotions with every kind of retailer abound. It could be gas stations, drug stores, or supermarkets. Or you buy a certain product and you get a free companion airline ticket. When you receive your monthly airline or credit card statement, any new promotions will be included. You can also find them on their websites.

Airline Partnership Programs: Most frequent flyer programs have agreements with other airlines from which you can collect and redeem miles. For example: American Airlines AAdvantage, the largest program, has a partnership with: Aer Lingus, Air Pacific, Air Tahiti, Alaskan, British Airways, Cathay Pacific, Finnair, Iberia, Japan Airlines, Lot Polish, Swiss Airlines, El Al, Asiana, Qantas, Turkish Airlines, and others. Verify with American Advantage whether you can accrue on all flights or only specific routings, and whether you can redeem miles on the other airline. The programs vary and change constantly.

Benefits of Frequent Flyer Miles

- ***This is best for people with money and people who are frequent travelers.***

If you travel a lot, then you are familiar with the benefits of collecting frequent flyer miles. These programs are really designed with the frequent traveler in mind. You need to be on airplanes quite frequently to have these programs pay off. If you are a once-a-year traveler and pay off your credit cards with only the minimum balance each month, then these programs are not for you.

For example: If you travel once a year from NYC to Los Angeles and purchase a nonrefundable airline ticket, it will take you more than 5 years to get enough miles for a free trip, and this is assuming the number of miles for a free ticket remains 25,000. If they increase it, it will take you longer. If you use an American Airlines Advantage credit card and do NOT pay your bill off each month, your monthly finance fee could add up to

For the latest information about frequent flyer programs send an e-mail to *tips@discounttravelwisdom.com* more than the price of a purchased airline ticket. It wouldn't make sense financially to participate in a frequent flyer mileage program.

Best Use of Your Frequent Flyer Miles

In my opinion, the best use of frequent flyer miles is to redeem them for an upgrade. You may have to purchase a more expensive ticket than you planned, but the chance to fly in business class or first class should not be missed, especially if you have never flown up front.

For example: You want to fly NYC to Paris on Delta in June. The summer **economy** fare is approximately $850, depending on when you purchase your ticket, what your travel dates are, and what is available at the time. To get this same ticket for free (but you must pay a few fees—security fee and others) you will use **50,000**[4] of your Delta "Skymiles," assuming you've met all the rules.

Just as a quirk, you ask the agent how many miles it would take to **UPGRADE TO BUSINESS CLASS**. It is **40,000** miles round-trip from **selected** economy class fares. On your travel dates, the least expensive economy fare valid for upgrade is approximately $1,300, an additional $450 over the fare you would have paid anyway, and you save 10,000 miles. You've always wanted to go to Paris, and this is your splurge trip, so the additional money will be budgeted in.

But the real glory of this upgrade is how much money you have saved. If you were to buy a roundtrip business class ticket from NYC to Paris and back, the airfare would be approximately **$6,400**! You would be saving over **$5,000** to travel in business class.

Obviously, collecting 40,000 miles could be a stretch. If you don't fly much, this means spending over $40,000 on your Delta/American Express Skymiles credit card. Or you could take some Delta flights within the U.S. The longer the flight, the more miles you collect.

Every time you fly, the ticket you purchased was based on the "air miles" (miles counted in a straight line, i.e., as a crow flies) between the two cities you are flying. These "air miles" are the same as the frequent flyer miles you accrue. JFK/NYC to Los Angeles is 2,459 air miles one way, 4,918 miles roundtrip. To get 40,000, you would have to fly 9 roundtrips.

[4] Mileage awards as of November 2002.

How to Redeem Your Miles

These are general guidelines. Every airline processes their frequent flyer awards differently. The steps involved vary by airline, but this is the basic information you will need. What follows are the things you need to do and the key questions you need to ask.

Your Steps

1. Find out if you have enough miles.
2. Check for frequent flyer seat availability.
3. Make reservation.
4. Order award coupon.
5. Redeem award coupon against airline reservation.
6. Ask for a written confirmation.
7. Review written confirmation for accuracy.
8. Do some research about your destination.

Have This Stuff Handy

- Your current frequent flyer statement (you can get a copy off the airline's website)
- Pin number
- Circle or highlight your frequent flyer number and total number of miles you have earned
- A credit card to pay for taxes, security charges or expedite fees
- Have airline frequent flyer telephone number ready
- Have completely thought out your travel guidelines: travel dates, who is going, where you are going. Have a back-up plan and dates Or you could ask them what dates are available in a 7-day range
- Calendar, pen and large sheets of paper
- Set aside at least one hour to do research. Hopefully it won't take that long

Step One: Do You Have Enough Miles?

See Figure 15.1 for Frequent Flyer Steps fill-in sheet.

CALL the airline frequent flyer telephone number or go on line. (Personally, I'd call. Too much can go wrong.) Pay attention to the menu recordings and go to the right department. Otherwise, you could get someone not familiar with frequent flyer transactions. Make sure you go to the domestic desk for flights within the U.S. and go to the international desk for flights outside the U.S. If you travel a lot and have an "elite" frequent flyer status, you will want to use the special number the airline gave you. The more savvy reservation agents work at the elite desks. They may also have promotions only for their better customers.

Ask These Questions

First Determine Whether You Have Enough Miles. The information on the statement you have may, or may not, be accurate. You may have an old statement that does not reflect recent purchases or flights. Statements are only mailed out periodically and only if you have some kind of activity on it. Look up your account online to get current information.

Write on Top of Your Paper

(or use the Figure 15.1 fill-in sheet):

Date ________________

AIRLINE ________________ Freq Flyer #____________________

Phone __________________________ Pin # ________________

Number of miles in your account ________________________

How many miles does it take for one person to fly?

From/airport ___________ to destination/airport _____________

Miles __________________ award code ___________________

What are the blackout dates for this award? ______________

Blackout dates are dates the fare or award is not valid. If there are blackout dates for the above award and you are not flexible with your dates, **ask:**

- If there is a different award that would apply for your specific dates. If they offer one, it is probably double the number of miles of the other award and offered on most economy seats on the plane.

Number of miles ______________ Award code ______________

- **Do I have enough miles for one person to fly on the dates I want, enough for 2, or however many? Ask if there are any specials or companion awards.**

Ask the agent what letter your award is booked in. You probably won't see it anywhere (except on the airline ticket), but it will make it easier to double-check the information during a future phone call.

TIP: If you have to call back, compare the number of miles, the award code and the special inventory to the new information. There are so many awards and interpretations that quite often you are given incorrect information.

A Word About Frequent Flyer Inventory

Now that you know you have enough miles, you are ready to check the availability for the frequent flyer seats. The inventory used is different from the inventory used for paying tickets. There are far fewer seats allotted to frequent flyer space, and they can be difficult to find, especially over school vacations and holidays—SO PLAN FAR IN ADVANCE.

Step Two: Check Seat Availability

With travel dates in hand:

ASK the reservation agent to check for flights with available frequent flyer seats. It may take some time to find seats, so be prepared.

WRITE down on your large sheet of paper the times and flight numbers of **available** flights, in case you have a choice.

Departing Flight Outbound date:

From ____________________ to ____________________

Flight number ____________

Departs at ________________ from airport ____________

Arrives at ________________ airport ________________

If you are changing planes enroute:

From ____________________ to ____________________

Flight number ____________

Departs at ________________ from airport ____________

Arrives at ________________ airport ________________

For return flight: Return date:

From ____________________ to ____________________

Flight number ____________

Departs at ________________ from airport ____________

Arrives at ________________ airport ________________

If you are changing planes enroute:
From ______________________ to ______________________
Flight number ______________
Departs at __________________ from airport ______________
Arrives at __________________ airport ____________________

Step Three: Make Your Reservation

Book the number of seats you need to match the number of awards you will be ordering.

Give the **Legal Names** of the travelers—the name that matches frequent flyer account and your identification.

Write flight information: When the agent reads you the confirmed reservation, make sure you have written the information down correctly.

Listen: pay close attention to the agent when she recaps your reservation. Immediately make any necessary corrections, especially with dates or spelling of the names.

Make Note of the Ticketing Date: Every airline has different rules on when the award reservation must be ticketed. The airline reservation will be automatically cancelled by the airline's computer system if a ticket number is not added to the reservation by the ticketing deadline date. So HIGHLIGHT IT, CIRCLE IT, PUT A STICKY NOTE ON YOUR DESK, ON YOUR REFRIGERATOR AND ON YOUR BATHROOM MIRROR to avoid losing this reservation.

Make Note of Your Reservation Number, also known as your confirmation number. You will need this to assist the next reservation agent in finding your frequent flyer airline reservation.

While you are still on the phone with the reservation agent,

Ask: Do I need to order the award certificate?

- If yes, and you are ready to finalize your trip, ask to be transferred immediately to that department and take care of it.
- If not, ask whether they can add the award to your reservation (electronically) now? If so, do it now.

A NOTE: If you are not yet ready to finalize your trip, just make the reservation and note ticketing date. You can call back and order the certificate when your plans are firm, but it must be done prior to the airline ticketing deadline. **SEE STEP FOUR**, the next step, before you hang up with reservations.

Step Four: Order Your Award Coupon

This is not an obvious step. Many people assume that making a frequent flyer airline reservation is all you need to do to use your miles. NOT SO. Once you have determined whether you have enough miles and made your airline reservation, you still need to order the award and have the ticket issued. Unfortunately, the reservation agent does not tell you that you still need to order the award and redeem it against your airline reservation. The reservation agent's job is done when the airline reservation has been confirmed and the award code information has been added to reservation. YOU MUST BE AWARE THAT YOU ARE NOT YET FINISHED. THE AWARD STILL NEEDS TO BE ORDERED AND THE TICKET ISSUED.

Ask the Reservation Agent: How do I redeem my miles? They will either:

1. Transfer you to the appropriate department to order the award certificate (call back if you get cut off.)

OR

2. Immediately take the miles out of your frequent flyer account and add them to your reservation. No coupon is issued. The award information is added to your reservation "electronically." This will also immediately ISSUE your airline ticket, making you subject to revision fees.

If You Need to Order Your Frequent Flyer Award

Speak to the Department that sends them out. This could be called customer service, the award redemption department, or something else.

Ask How Long It Will Take to Get the Award Certificate: If you are traveling more that a month away, you could go the snail mail route. If you are traveling within the next week, you'll have to use the "expedite" service, if they have one.

Snail Mailed Certificates: These are paper certificates that are mailed to you in advance. You can order them far in advance, especially when you know you will need them but your dates aren't set yet. When you receive them, put them in a safe place; they are very difficult to replace. There is no fee for snail mailed certificates.

Expedite Service: These are paper certificates that are sent via an overnight service such as FedEx. This is offered for those last-minute folks. The fees vary, between $20 and $100 per certificate. They may also offer an "electronic certificate" with a higher service fee. This is an electronic message that is attached to your airline reservation. Plan far in advance to avoid these high fees.

Ask What Kind of Award Document Is Issued: Depending on when you are ordering, your award could be either a PAPER certificate that needs to be mailed to you and then redeemed for your airline ticket, or it could be an "electronic ticket award," a computer message added to your reservation.

If an "Electronic Award" Is Issued: It was probably processed while you were on the phone making the airline reservation. The only way you know that this was done is by the itinerary you receive. Hopefully it will state that an electronic ticket was issued and will have the ticket numbers on the itinerary.

If a Paper Award Certificate Is Sent: If you chose to have your award snail-mailed, it will probably take 7–10 days to show up. Watch your mailbox for it. If you have not received it in 10 days, call the award department to make sure it was actually sent out. I don't know how many times I've had this happen, so I usually advise my client that it has been "expedited for a fee" so we will get it faster. This way, I don't forget about it and it doesn't snowball into a monster mess. ONCE YOU RECEIVE THE AWARD CERTIFICATE, IT MUST BE REDEEMED FOR THE AIRLINE TICKET.

Step Five: Redeem Award Certificate and Issue Airline Ticket

Once you receive your paper award certificate, you must then take it to either a city ticket counter or the airport to have the ticket issued against the certificate. Only the frequent flyer member or the name on the certificate can do this. You can't send your assistant or friend to redeem. You will have to show a picture identification that matches the name on the coupon to redeem. Bring your confirmation number and flight information with you. This will help the agent find your reservation and issue your airline ticket.

NOTE: Once the award certificate is issued, it must be redeemed within one year. Once a ticket is issued against an award certificate, that ticket is valid for one year, subject to revision fees.

Step Six: Written Confirmation of Itinerary

When you have finished all of the above steps, you should receive some type of written confirmation. It could be a mailed itinerary, a faxed copy, or an email. If you have received it by computer, print out a copy.

Step Seven: Look Over the Itinerary Immediately

I have given this a separate step to emphasize how very important this is. **YOU ABSOLUTELY MUST IMMEDIATELY LOOK OVER YOUR ITINERARY.** Also, show it to anyone else traveling with you. A second pair of eyes may catch a mistake that you have overlooked.

- ***Any mistake you find at this point will be very difficult to fix and may cost you extra money.***

If you find an error, call the airline immediately and explain the difficulty. Hopefully, you will be able to have it fixed. You will be subject to the rules again, i.e., mileage award, blackout dates, routings, seat availability and ticket reissue fee, if necessary. Have your credit card ready. There probably will be fees to pay, and you may have to return to the ticket counter to have it fixed.

What to Look For on Your Itinerary

- Spelling of all names
- Dates and times of travel
- Departure airport and destination city/airport
- AIRLINE TICKET NUMBER: This is your proof that the award certificate has been redeemed for an airline ticket. It may say at the top, "This is your confirmation for your electronic ticket" or something similar. If you do not see the ticket number, call the airline and ask reservations to look in your reservation for your ticket number. Then write the numbers on the itinerary or ask the airline to send you a new itinerary with the ticket numbers on it.

Changing Dates and Cities After the Certificate Is Redeemed

You may be able to change your dates at this point, but you have to follow all the rules again, i.e., blackout dates, seat availability, and routing. Your ticket may need to be reissued, so another trip to the ticket counter might be necessary. Most airlines charge a fee to change an award ticket.

Unused Award Certificate and Ticket

If for some reason you are unable to travel on this award ticket, you can return it to the airline and redeposit the miles into your frequent flyer account. Most airlines charge a fee for this, approximately $50 to $100.

Tips for Collecting and Redeeming Your Miles

- Collect miles only on one airline.
- Obtain that airline's credit card and pay off the balance monthly to avoid high interest rates.
- Chose an airline that serves your local airport.
- If you have a specific vacation destination in mind, be sure your choice of airline flies there or has a partner airline that does.
- Check with your airline's frequent flyer department to find out how many miles you will need.
- Plan school vacation and summer travel 6 to 9 months in advance to have a better chance with seat availability.
- The total miles you need must be in your account before you plan your trip. The airline will not make a reservation if you don't have enough miles.

If You Have Access to the Web

- Look up your confirmed reservation online. Verify that the information given to you was what you wrote down.
- Look up the awards and read the rules.
- See if there are any award promotions that the agent may have missed.
- Once your reservation has been ticketed by the frequent flyer department look at your confirmation and see whether there are ticket numbers on it. Hopefully you have received an email or faxed confirmation.

Noteworthy Tips

Several airlines have **either reduced or eliminated black-out dates** on award travel, but inventory is still capacity controlled and will be difficult to get if not booked far in advance. You can book as far as 330 days in advance on some of the larger airlines. United Airlines has added a special capacity controlled inventory for their very frequent flyers. This inventory is not available to the general traveling public.

FIGURE 15.1

Frequent Flyer Steps

Date ____________

Airline ____________ Phone # ____________ Freq Flyer # ____________

Number of miles in account ____________ Pin # ____________

STEP 1: how many miles does it take for one person to fly? Do I have enough?

From/airport ____________ to destination city ____________

Number of miles needed for roundtrip ____________ Economy ________ Upgrade ________ F/C ________

award code ____________

What are the blackout dates for this award? ____________

Blackout dates are dates the fare or award is not valid. If there are blackout dates for the above award and you are not flexible with your dates, **ask** how many miles it will take to fly desired dates.

STEP 2: Check seat/award availability:

OUTBOUND FLIGHT INFORMATION

Date:	________	Day	________
Airline	________	Flight #	________
From	________	Time	________
Arr.Arpt	________	Time	________
If Conx A/L	________	Flight #	________
Dptr.Arpt	________	Time	________
Arr.Arpt	________	Time	________

RETURN FLIGHT INFORMATION

Date:	________	Day	________
Airline	________	Flight #	________
From	________	Time	________
Arr.Arpt	________	Time	________
If Conx A/L	________	Flight #	________
Dptr.Arpt	________	Time	________
Arr.Arpt	________	Time	________

STEP 3: Make reservation: confirmation number ____________

STEP 4: Order award certificate: 1. Coupon/cert ordered ________ Date ________

2. No cert needed, electronic certificate issued ________ Date ________

STEP 5: Redeem award, ticket issued ________ Date ________

STEP 6: Review written confirmation for accuracy ________ Date ________

Appendix

Glossary—Industry Lingo 239
Hotel Phone Numbers and Websites 245
Car Phone Numbers and Websites 247
Ordering Information 248
Vacation Request Form 249

GLOSSARY

Industry Lingo

ADJOINING ROOMS: rooms that have a shared wall between them but not a door that opens.

ALL-INCLUSIVE: a misnomer these days. Usually refers to everything being included in the one price you have prepaid—airfare, hotel, transfers, food, drink, entertainment, limited sports, taxes and service charges. Now it's not so all-inclusive. Additional fees may apply to motorized sports or name-brand booze. Read the fine print in the brochure or ask the booking agent what additional charges might apply.

AP: AMERICAN PLAN: at a hotel, 3 meals a day priced as one flat amount. Usually has a children's rate. Add taxes and service charge to this amount.

APEX: term used for advance purchase excursion fare. Almost always non-refundable and restrictive.

ATO: airport ticket counter.

AVAILABILITY: the controlling of inventory in a specific manner.

B & B: BED AND BREAKFAST: usually old homes converted into small hotels that serve breakfast.

BP: BERMUDA PLAN: also known as breakfast plan. Full or buffet breakfast is included in nightly hotel rate.

BLACKOUTS: dates that an airfare, hotel or car rates are not offered for sale. Must pay a higher rate.

BUCKET: a category of inventory. Every flight has a variety of prices offered for sale. Each price is represented in availability by a letter of the alphabet. Each letter is a bucket and has a specific number of seats in that category. When it is empty, that airfare category or bucket is sold out and no longer offered for sale on that flight. Hotels and car companies have also instituted this same pricing strategy.

CAPACITY CONTROLLED INVENTORY: the availability of specific rates has a limited number of seats, rooms or cars offered at that price. When that number (or bucket) is exceeded, that rate is no longer offered for sale.

CDW: COLLISION DAMAGE WAIVER/LOSS-DAMAGE WAIVER: a sneaky way for the car rental companies to make extra money. Not an insurance, this coverage protects you from paying big bucks if you damage the car. Most renters have coverage through other sources such as credit card benefits or car owner's insurance.

CHANGE OF GAUGE: a flight that makes a stop and changes the aircraft used. Sold as one flight number with one flight coupon. Listed in the computer and on your itinerary as "1" stop. Complicates ticketing and seat assignments.

CRS: COMPUTER RESERVATION SYSTEM: or GDS: GLOBAL DISTRIBUTION SYSTEM: the computer system used by travel agents and other travel companies. It contains airline flight schedules with availability and prices as well as other travel related products such as hotels, car rentals, tours and cruises.

CODE SHARING: a marketing gimmick. Two airlines sell seats on the same aircraft. This flight is listed in the computer of both airlines and listed in the CRS that travel agents use with both airlines' flight numbers. The flight may be sold out on one airline and available on the other. Fares for the same seat/flight may vary. Host airline tends to be cheaper.

CONNECTING ROOMS: rooms that share a wall and have a door that opens between them.

CONSOLIDATOR: a company that buys a product such as airline tickets in bulk and sells them at a discount. Usually heavily restricted.

CONTINENTAL PLAN: hotel rate that may include continental breakfast.

CB: CONTINENTAL BREAKFAST: usually includes bread of some type, cereals, fruit, juice, coffee or tea. Does not include the hot stuff like bacon and eggs. Depends on what the restaurant is serving.

CTO: airline city ticket office.

DEREGULATION: stupid government tricks. Government gets out of overseeing the airline industry: 1978 Airline Deregulation Act. Originally intended to spur growth and competition as in "no frills" discount airlines. Now it's Darwin's theory modified—survival of the biggest pocketbooks.

DEMI-PENSION: breakfast included in hotel rate. Hotel rates are frequently quoted this way internationally.

DEPARTURE TAX: another tax. This one levied by a country as you leave it. Sometimes you have prepaid this tax on your airline ticket; sometimes you have to pay it in local currency as you leave the country. Ask when purchasing your ticket.

DIRECT FLIGHT: a flight that makes a stop enroute. Passengers need not get off. This is NOT a term for a nonstop flight. Listed in the computer and on your itinerary as "1" stop.

DOT: U.S. Department of Transportation. Bureaucracy at its finest.

DROP-OFF CHARGE: the fee charged by a car rental company for picking up a car in one location and returning it to another.

ELECTRONIC TICKET: the ticket information, flights and fare paid are stored in the reservation in the form of a computer message.

FAA: Federal Aviation Administration. www.faa.gov

FAMILY PLAN: sometimes traveling with family members may entitle you to a discount. Not very common with airfares but more so with hotels, cruises and tours.

EP: EUROPEAN PLAN: nothing included in room rate.

FAP: FULL AMERICAN PLAN: see American plan.

GUARANTEED RESERVATION: a reservation that is confirmed only when a credit card is given or prepayment is sent. It protects the hotel from lost revenue when a guest does not arrive, especially on a sold-out night. The credit card is usually charged the one night plus tax, or the prepayment is forfeited.

IN-HOUSE: within a company.

INTERLINE: traveling or transferring baggage from one airline to another.

LOAD FACTOR: the number of passengers carried on a flight.

MANIFEST: a list of names on a flight.

MCO: miscellaneous charge order. Used by travel agents and airlines for travel related charges. An accountable document like an airline ticket, that cannot be replaced if lost.

MINIMUM CONNECTING TIME: the time an airline has determined it takes for a passenger to change from one flight to another and for their bags to be switched from one flight to another. This time frame is a guideline for booking reservations and gives the airline an excuse to not compensate you if you book flights too close together (under the minimum published connecting time) and you miss your connecting flight.

MAP: MODIFIED AMERICAN PLAN: at a hotel, 2 meals a day, usually breakfast and dinner, priced as one flat amount, plus tax and service charge. Usually has a children's rate.

NONSTOP FLIGHT: a flight that goes from one point to another without stopping. Listed in the computer and on your itinerary as "0" stops or nonstop.

NO-SHOW: when you have a confirmed reservation and do not use it. With hotel bookings usually there is a one night's charge applied to the credit card used to "guarantee" the reservation. Airlines do not charge for no-shows, except with nonrefundable airfares—"use it or lose it" fares.

OPEN JAW: refers to the type of routing on a roundtrip airline ticket. You arrive in one city and depart from a different city, i.e., you arrive in Los Angeles and depart from San Francisco.

OUT-SOURCED: a project is given to an outside company to produce.

PAPER TICKET: the new terminology for the old-fashioned ticket made out of paper. This is to distinguish the new computer ticket message/electronic ticket from the old- fashioned thing you carried in your hand. Should be phased out by 2004.

PAX: an industry abbreviation for passenger.

PNR: passenger name record. This is the computer file that contains all the information pertaining to your airline reservation.

PNR NUMBER: the computer reference number, reservation number or confirmation number for an airline reservation. Also known as the RECORD LOCATOR.

RACK RATE: the suggested retail price of a hotel room. Rarely should you pay this. There is always a way to get a discount, sometimes by just asking.

RECORD LOCATOR: see PNR NUMBER.

RESERVATION NUMBER: i.e., confirmation number. The identifying number attached to a reservation. This is usually proof that you are confirmed on something.

REVENUE: the amount of money expected to be earned from selling a product.

REVENUE PASSENGER MILES: the amount of money earned from one paying passenger carried one mile.

RULE 240: the governing tariff rule that gives an airline the latitude to reroute you and reissue your ticket without cost.

SEAT PITCH: on an aircraft seat, the distance between the front of your seat and the back of the one in front of you.

SLOTS: 1. Time parameters established for the take off and landing of airplanes at an airport. For example, American has hourly time slots 7 A.M., 8 A.M., 9 A.M., etc. for departing flights between LaGuardia and O'Hare. 2. One-armed bandits.

SNAIL MAIL: U.S. POSTAL SERVICE. Since the advent of the Internet and email, stuff sent via the post office now seems to take forever, or as slow as a snail.

STANDBY: or space available: the "wait and see" of the airline biz. Once confirmed passengers have boarded a flight, any remaining seats can be offered to those folks waiting to get on but who do not have a reservation. This convenience is being phased out for nonrefundable airfares.

TICKET: a piece of paper or electronic message that says you have paid for a product. Usually states what you have purchased and when it is valid.

"USE IT OR LOSE IT": usually refers to a nonrefundable airline ticket. The ticket is only valid for travel on the flights and dates written on the ticket. If unused, value is forfeited.

VAT—Value Added Tax: akin to a luxury tax levied by governments to soak the visitor. Supposed to pay for tourism promotion and travel-related stuff. Can be reimbursable by the foreign government.

W/C: water closet, loo, toilet, lavatory, rest room or bathroom.

YIELD MANAGEMENT: the highly evolved system that determines pricing per item depending on a variety of factors. For example, how many seats sold at a discount will vary depending on that flight's revenue expectations.

Hotel Phone Numbers and Websites

RATING	NAME	PHONE	WEBSITE	AFFILIATION
First/Business	Adams Mark	800-444-ADAM	*adamsmark.com*	
Varies/Intl	Accor	800-221-4542	*accorhotel.com*	Accor
Economy/Busi.	Amerisuites	800-833-1516	*Amerisuites.com*	
Varies/resort	Aston (Hawaii)	800-922-7866	*Astonhotels.com*	
Economy/suites	Baymont Inns and Suites	800-301-0200	*baymontinns.com*	
Economy	Best Western Hotels	800-780-7234	*bestwestern.com*	
First/Suites	Candlewood	888-226-3539	*candlewoodsuites.com*	
Economy	Choice	800-424-6423	*choicehotels.com*	Choice
Economy	Clarion	800-252-7466	*choicehotels.com*	Choice
Economy	Comfort Inn and Suites	800-517-4000	*comfortsuites.com*	
Luxury	Conrad	800-HILTONS	*Hilton.com*	Hilton
Moderate	Courtyard by Marriott	800-321-2211	*courtyard.com*	Marriott
First/Business	Crown Plaza	800-2CROWNE	*crownplaza.com*	
Economy	Days Inn	800-329-7466	*daysinn.com*	
First/Business	Doubletree	800-222-8733		Hilton
Economy	Econo Lodge	800-424-6423	*choicehotels.com*	Choice
First/Business	Embassy Suites	800-362-8300		Hilton
Economy/suites	Fairfield Inn and Suites	800-228-2800	*marriott.com*	Marriott
Deluxe/Luxury	Fairmont Hotels	800-441-1414	*fairmont.com*	Fairmont
Moderate	Four Points by Sheraton	800-325-3535	*sheraton.com*	starwood
Luxury	Four Seasons	800-332-3442	*fourseasons.com*	
Economy	Hampton Inns	800-426-7866		Hilton
Moderate/Suites	Hawthorn Suites	800-527-1133	*hawthorn.com*	
Varies/First/DLX	Hilton Hotels	800-HILTONS	*Hilton.com*	Hilton
Moderate/Varies	Holiday Inns	800-HOLIDAY	*holidayinn.com*	6 Continents Hotels

RATING	NAME	PHONE	WEBSITE	AFFILIATION
Moderate/Suites	Homewood Suites	800-225-5466	*Homewood-suites.com*	Hilton
Economy	Howard Johnson's	800-446-4656	*hojo.com*	
First/Deluxe	Hyatt Hotels	800-233-1234	*hyatt.com*	
Deluxe/Luxury	InterContinental Hotels	800-327-0200	*interconti.com*	
First	Loews Hotels	800-235-6395	*loewshotels.com*	
Economy?	MainStay Suites	800-660-6246	*mainststaysuites.com*	
Deluxe	Marriott Hotels	800-238-9290	*marriott.com*	
Economy	Motel 6	800-466-8356	*motel6.com*	
Luxury	Peninsula Hotels	800-262-9467	*peninsula.com*	Starwood
Economy	Quality Inns and Suites	800-228-5151	*qualityinn.com*	
First	Radisson Hotels	800-333-3333	*radisson.com*	
Economy	Ramada Inn and Suites	800-228-2828	*ramadahotels.com*	
Economy	Red Roof Inns	800-733-7663	*redroof.com*	
Luxury	Regent International	800-545-4000	*fourseasons.com*	Four Seasons
First/Deluxe	Renaissance Hotels	800-468-3571	*renaissancehotels.com*	
Luxury	Ritz Carlton Hotels	800-241-3333	*ritzcarlton.com*	
First/Deluxe	Sheraton Hotels	888-625-5144	*sheraton.com*	Starwood
Moderate	Sierra Suites and Hotels	800-474-3772	*sierrasuites.com*	
Moderate	Springhill Suites	888-228-9290	*springhillsuites.com*	
Deluxe/Luxury	Starwood Hotels	888-625-5144	*starwoodhotels.com*	
First	Summerfield Suites	800-996-3426	*wyndham.com*	Wyndham
Economy	Super 8	800-800-8000	*super8.com*	
Economy	Town Place Suites	800-228-9290	*townplace.com*	
Economy	Travelodge	800-578-7878	*travelodge.com*	
Deluxe	Westin Hotels	800-625-5144	*westin.com*	Starwood
First	Wyndham Hotels	800-996-3426	*wyndham.com*	

Car Rental Phone Numbers and Websites

NAME	PHONE	WEBSITE
ALAMO	800-GOALAMO	*goalamo.com*
AUTOEUROPE	800-223-5555	*autoeurope.com*
AVIS	800-331-2121	*avis.com*
BUDGET	800-527-0700	*budget.com*
DOLLAR	800-800-4000	*dollar.com*
ENTERPRISE	800-325-8007	*enterprise.com*
HERTZ	800-645-3131	*hertz.com*
KEMWEL	800-678-0678	*kemwel.com*
NATIONAL	800-468-3334	*national.com*
PAYLESS	800-541-1566	*paylesscarrental.com*
THRIFTY	800-THRIFTY	*thrifty.com*

Ordering Information

PRODUCT	PRICE		QTY		SUBTOTAL
Paperback: ***Discount Travel Wisdom***	$19.95	x	____	=	______
Bulk purchase, e-mail for price		x	____	=	______
SEMINAR: "The Art of Discount Travel":					
CD	49.95	x	____	=	______
Double Tape Cassettes:	39.95	x	____	=	______
OTHER ____________________	$ _____	x	____	=	______
Shipping and handling: $3.00 per item	$3.00	x	____	=	______
				TOTAL:	______

Guarantee: Everything we sell comes with a money back, lifetime guarantee. If you are not happy, send it back!

Name ____

Address ____

City ________________________ State ______ Zip ________

Phone ________________ Email __________________________

❑ VISA ❑ MC ❑ AM EX ❑ Personal check (payable to Elaine Ktistes)

Acct No. ______________________________ Exp. Date _______

Signature _____________________________ Date ________

(Credit card charges will appear as K Travel Advisors)

OR ORDER ONLINE AT *www.discounttravelwisdom.com*

Please send this form along with your check or credit card information to: K Travel Press, P.O. Box 4705, Long Island City, NY 11104.

Vacation Request Form

Contact information:
Name ______________________ Day phone ______________
Address ______________________________________
Home phone ______________
City ______________________ State/zip ______________

(1) Names/Ages ______________________________________
____
____

(2) Departure date______________ return date ______________
Departure airport ______________ departure airport ______________
More than one city? ______________

(3) Desired destination(s) ______________________________
Hotel name ______________________ number of nights ________
Hotel quality level: ❑ economy ❑ moderate ❑ deluxe ❑ other______________
How will you use your hotel? ❑ sleep only ❑ sleep and swim ❑ sleep,swim,play

(4) What activities do you want to do when you get there? ______________
____
Have you been there before? ❑ yes ❑ no If yes, when? ______________
Why do you want to go there?______________________________
What do you want included in price: ______________________
❑ meals B L D ❑ all inclusive ❑ sightseeing/tour
car rental: size car ❑ Compact ❑ Midsize ❑ Fullsize ❑ transfers
❑ other features ______________________________
Can you commit to a prepaid package? ❑ Y ❑ N
Are your dates definite? ❑ Y ❑ N
What advertising has interested you? ______________________
Where did you go on your last vacation ______________________
What did you like best about it ______________________
What did you like least about it ______________________
What frequent flyer programs do you belong to?______________

(5) What is your estimated budget?______________________
Which credit card will you use?
Name/Number ______________________ Exp Date ________
Name on cc ______________________ CID NBR ________
I understand that an itinerary planning fee of $150.00 will be charged to my credit card. This fee is for consulting and advise only and is NOT refundable nor can it be applied to my trip cost.

SIGN HERE ______________________ DATE ________

please email to: res@DiscountTravelWisdom.com

About the Author

Elaine Ktistes, CTC, is widely recognized as a leading expert on travel planning and finding travel discounts. She is a Certified Travel Counselor (the travel industry version of a CPA), member of ICTA and a "SABRE Master." As a travel agent for over 30 years, she has handled all types of travel and specializes in upscale travel, groups, and corporate travel. She has advised thousands of clients with travel planning, matching them to products that suit their needs. Ktistes regularly saves her clients from making costly errors, and saves them time and money.

In addition to travel planning, Ms. Ktistes has conducted travel seminars for both the general public, through the Learning Annex, and corporate seminars, through the travel agencies she has worked with.

Discount Travel Wisdom is her first book.